Date: 1/3/20

305.8927 ALD
Al-Deen, Aminah,
History of Arab Americans :
exploring diverse roots /

History of Arab Americans

History of Arab Americans

Exploring Diverse Roots

Aminah Al-Deen

 GREENWOOD™

An Imprint of ABC-CLIO, LLC
Santa Barbara, California • Denver, Colorado

Library of Congress Cataloging-in-Publication Data

Names: Al-Deen, Aminah, author.
Title: History of Arab Americans : exploring diverse roots / Aminah Al-Deen.
Description: Santa Barbara, California : Greenwood, An Imprint of ABC-CLIO, LLC,
   2019. | Includes bibliographical references and index.
Identifiers: LCCN 2018032076 | ISBN 9781440840692 (eBook) |
   ISBN 9781440840685 (cloth : alk. paper)
Subjects: LCSH: Arab Americans—History.
Classification: LCC E184.A65 A42 2019 | DDC 305.892/7073—dc23
LC record available at https://lccn.loc.gov/2018032076

ISBN: 978-1-4408-4068-5 (print)
       978-1-4408-4069-2 (ebook)

23 22 21 20 19   1 2 3 4 5

This book is also available as an eBook.

Greenwood
An Imprint of ABC-CLIO, LLC

ABC-CLIO, LLC
130 Cremona Drive, P.O. Box 1911
Santa Barbara, California 93116-1911
www.abc-clio.com

This book is printed on acid-free paper ∞

Manufactured in the United States of America

To the wonderful grandkids—Jennah, Nasir, Ruby, Yaeli, and Toussaint. May you read this one day.

Contents

Introduction

Why is a history of Arab Americans important? Today in the 21st century, one description of who they are (terrorists or potential terrorists) and another description of when they came (in the latter part of the 20th century) dominate. Both of these descriptors are patently wrong. This text will explore Arab American culture, what influenced Arabs to come to the United States before and after it became a nation, and their immigrant and citizen experiences in the 20th century. The text will also explore their presence in various media and after the events of September 11, 2001.

Who are Arabs, as distinct from others living in the Middle East? They are first mentioned in the mid-ninth century BCE as a tribal people dwelling on the land that came to be called the central Arabian Peninsula. They were under the loose governance of a series of empires, including the Roman and Sassanian Empires. Further description of Arabs, however, requires a distinction between religious, geographic, cultural, and linguistic definitions.

The Religious Definition

Islamic tradition holds that Arabs are the descendants of Ishmael, son of Abraham, but one must then account for Arab Christians and Jews who do not hold Ishmael in their lineage. Jews are the descendants of Abraham's other son, Isaac, so Arab Jews and Muslims are considered cousins. Christians are not Abraham's descendants by blood but inherited portions of the Jewish tradition through Jesus Christ, who is seen as a rabbi.

The Geographic Definition

If the definition of who is Arab is purely by location, researchers are on much safer ground. An Arab is one descended from those who lived in a certain place in recorded history. This text uses a geographical approach, since the values and moral norms predominating in the region transcend religious traditions.

Is there one Arab culture, given the diversity of 22 countries? Is there really an Arab world? And is "Arab" culture monolithic? Geographically, what is called the Arab world is mostly uninhabited desert. For comparison, the Sudan is larger than Western Europe but has a 10th the population. Saudi Arabia is bigger than Texas and Alaska combined, and Egypt is 95 percent desert. The topography of the land accounts for some distinctions among countries. Natural land features, proximity to water, and differences in weather determine which animals and vegetables are plentiful. The natural features of the land also determine whether certain kinds of wood or other building materials are readily available.

The Cultural Approach: Beliefs and Values

Researchers can find information on a people's outlook on life and how their social behavior is arranged by examining general beliefs and practices. Here, some broad generalizations in a comparative mode may be helpful to readers. Americans generally believe that the individual is an essential focal point of social existence. This, however, is mediated by the importance of relationships of individuals in families, neighborhoods, workplaces, and so on. The role of law is especially important in America because the social arrangement is predicated on rights and privileges for citizens. Citizens, for example, have the right to privacy. These beliefs and the values that derive from them provide a position from which Americans see the world.

Arab Americans, on the other hand, come from collectivist cultures where it is the family that is the central focus. They generally believe that it is not the individual who is in control of most things in life. The controlling factor is God or fate. The individual is directly tied to the family and its successes and setbacks and functions as an integral part of that family dynamic. The issues of the rights and privileges of citizens was not a subject of discussion until contemporary times, given that Arabs in most prior times lived as subjects of empire. As subjects who were in essence owned by the ruler, they had little say in government and no say in policies that affected them except for provincial rulers appointed by the government.

Arabs eat different foods and have distinctive traditional manners of dress, housing, decorative arts, and architectural styles. Their politics also differ, as do the forms of government. There are monarchies, military governments, socialist republics, and now a few countries engaging in participatory democracy. Yet, their outlook on life has some similarities that cross national borders. In general, Arab societies are conservative and demand conformity as a rule. For example, many child-rearing practices are the same regardless of country, and there is a high regard for respecting tradition. After a millennia of experience with Islam, Muslims and non-Muslims alike have been culturally influenced by the religion.

Arabs as a whole, irrespective of class, value good manners at all times. Proper etiquette, deference to elders, and a respect for social ranking are central tenets. Reputation is highly valued and must be protected at all costs. Personal preference takes a backseat to loyalty to family and tribe. Social class and family background are often on display, determining personal status rather than individual character and personal achievement. Conservative social morality must be recognized and maintained. As a result, first meetings are among individuals of status. Most other Americans would agree with this set of values but with recognition of individual choice. As in other religiously conservative communities, conservative Islamic values and beliefs determine values and other views, and ideologies such as liberalism are not welcome.

The basic definition of friendship among Arabs is like that of the West—a relationship with someone whose company is frequent, sustained over long periods of time, and enjoyable. However, to this definition Arabs add duty explicitly, while for Westerners it is expected but implicit. Friends in the Arab world *must* help in times of need and do favors to the best of their ability (and a little beyond). Needless to say, friends are chosen especially carefully. Requests are rarely refused in an explicit negative manner, and every attempt is made to fulfill them.

Arabs see themselves as generous, hospitable, polite, and loyal (sometimes to a fault) to their families. Their civilization's contributions to the world are largely unrecognized in America, but Arabs themselves understand their contributions as proof of their historical global standing even though it has waned in past centuries.

In general, Arabs see themselves as victims of hostile Western colonizers and a continuing postcolonial propaganda war by the West.

The Linguistic Approach

A linguistic definition centers on the primary language of Arabic, but other Semitic languages (such as Aramaic and Hebrew) preceded Arabic in the region, and later colonial invasions brought a host of European languages. Most individuals speak in one of the dialects of Arabic, as it is the language of literature, the arts, and governments.

During the colonial period English, French, Italian, and Spanish were brought to the region, displacing the Semitic languages as languages of the educated and in some countries the language of government and literature. Multilinguistic urban centers were disconnected from the unlettered masses living in the countryside and other more rural areas. However, the Berbers, indigenous peoples of North Africa, protested the invasions of the Arab Muslims, were hostile to the incursions into their lands, and maintain tribal Berber languages to a great extent.

Arabs in America: The Historical Approach

A contextualizing historical approach addresses the cultural, political, and religious roots of Arabs in America that takes into consideration the history of their host.

Indeed, the history of Arabs in America is a complex story of people coming to the United States over the course of 100 years. Initially, at the end of the 19th century they came from the region variously known as Greater Syria or Mount Lebanon. They were predominantly Christian of a variety of ethnic Orthodox Christian communities, with a few Muslims who were both Sunni and Shia. All had lived under the Ottoman Empire, with their fate tied to a declining empire that was increasingly repressive to its Christian inhabitants regarding tax collection and land usurpation, leading some into a search for a new homeland. Arabs also came from several different economic classes, as evidenced by whether they could travel on steamships in first class or steerage.

No matter how they traveled, the voyages required extraordinary stamina. Food and medicines quickly ran out, as did patience. In steerage, people died quickly and had to be thrown overboard. Shipping merchants strived to make the most money possible per voyage; thus, ships were packed with people who had already traveled some distance to the few ports from where ships sailed to America.

The Eastern Seaboard of America to which Arab immigrants arrived seemed to be a bustling country coming into its own, with all sorts of opportunities for the hardworking and the entrepreneurial. Industrialization was emerging and factories were booming, as were small but growing companies that provided the needs of an ever-expanding population. This air of enterprise extended to the Midwest, with its endless factories and meatpacking plants. Still other Arab immigrants found the easygoing French patois of southern states such as Louisiana a pleasant place for resettlement, as France had a part in the various occupations of Lebanon.

Arab immigrants found that becoming naturalized citizens was a speedy process, only complicated by their place of origin and race. From the time of the Barbary Wars, tales of the Ottoman Empire had been augmented by accounts of missionaries traveling to the Muslim world to convert its subjects, painting a picture of barbaric peoples who lacked civilization. All were considered Muslim or hopelessly influenced by the "wicked" religion of Islam. Many Christians, realizing that the stereotype influenced the naturalization process, transitioned to Catholicism or Protestantism, while others quietly established Orthodox churches. Much of the early immigration of Orthodox Christians was supported by Protestant Christian societies.

This presented a problem for those Orthodox Christians whose immigration had not been supported by American societies. They had to prove they were Christian in immigration courts, which pressed them on their religion claims. Muslims had to prove that they were not a threat to the democratic land.

Arab Christian settlement in the United States was a relatively quiet affair. Many Arab Christians shortened or changed their names and moved to reestablish themselves in their new home but kept an eye toward the family members left behind and the brewing chaos in a declining Ottoman Empire. Arab-language newspapers appeared early in the 20th century to convey the events of Mount Lebanon as subjects began to decide whether to accept another colonization or seek freedom.

In the United States, rapid industrialization caused teeming cities, decay from pollution, and overcrowding as new immigrants outstripped available housing. Arab families with money found that they could buy some buildings and provide themselves with some income as they settled, while others were their tenants. World War I disrupted the lives of all natives and immigrants as men said goodbye to families to return to not so unfamiliar lands to fight. The women's suffrage movement was growing among women of means, and the population had to decide on a president to guide them through the war. Gearing up for the war, however, provided more work.

The Great Depression affected all families and shifted the industrial focus from luxury and military goods to providing almost nothing. The wealthy rented out rooms in their homes, while the less fortunate scavenged for food. Nevertheless, there was a real social bonding of people from many different lands, all experiencing the same trauma. There was no income to continue sending money to the homeland, and immigration slowed to a standstill.

One of the most important and enduring pictures of Arab Americans, painted in the 19th century, was that the lands of their origin were steeped in Islam (rather than a combination of Islam and Orthodox Christianity). The perception was that Arab immigrants were Muslim, and other roots were obscured. Though there is ample evidence of mockery as an aspect of the identities of Muslims and Islam, the fact that Arabs of the Orthodox Christian faith had been here since at least the 19th century went unnoticed. This fact can be explained simply by their almost complete integration into American society and a continuing American desire to place Islam "over there," never touching American soil.

Media coverage of events in the Middle East kept a Muslim face on the inhabitants, along with what became a stereotypical assessment of the men's moral fiber as cunning and sly. Arab women were seen as equally cunning and were depicted as such in blockbuster films of the 1960s. Essentially, Islam and its people were still "over there" and not likely to spread their vile ways to America.

The Civil Rights Act of 1964 and the Immigration and Nationality Act of 1965 changed the landscape, with more Arabs permitted entry into the United States. By this time, many Arab immigrants were Christian and Muslim Palestinians fleeing the Israeli takeover of their lands. The already established notion of Arabs as uncivilized awaited them; however, many integrated into major city life with little notice. By the time of the Iranian hostage crisis in 1979, all persons from the Middle East were considered Arab, including Iranians.

After the 1980s, the settlement of Arab Muslims was both much more difficult and much easier. Travel to the Middle East was opened, and families began sending members to Palestine to fulfill Israeli occupation of home/land requirements. This also meant that their communities became increasingly self-segregated. Teenagers and young adults began a tradition of spending at least some of their time annually in Palestine. While this was a disruption in either schooling or work, it also limited full integration into American society. What was happening between Israel and Palestine became a priority in the minds of all, including Arabs from other countries in the region.

The entrance of Arabs from countries other than Palestine and Syria was largely unseen. Today in the United States, Arabs come from 22 different countries. There is significant cultural and class diversity, along with some diversity of religious practices. There are Sunni, Shia, and Sufi Muslims and some historically disassociated and theologically radical groups such as the Druze. Though many sympathize with the Palestinian problem, it is not at the heart of their concerns, as their countries' problems with autocratic rule and lack of various freedoms are paramount.

Various media and governmental agencies have consciously or unconsciously made a monolith of these various communities, and thus they are all seen as responsible for the actions of a few born in the Middle East and abroad. The array of almost indistinguishable names for terrorist groups has further complicated matters for most other Americans. According to some American media, they are the same and are all against America, which is an innocent player in the conflict. Likewise, leaders in foreign terrorist groups have pronounced America an evil entity, and subsequently some Americans have held them to their word. Thus, it is incorrect that all Muslims, wherever they are, feel the same, just as it is incorrect that all Americans or all of American media feel the same. It is absolutely incorrect to say that only the followers of one of the Abrahamic faiths is responsible for all the world's terror.

The longevity of the presence of Arabs in America and the establishment of roots by small Arab communities for over 100 years did not "establish" Islam in America further than the practice of some Arabs of Islam. However, Arabs can speak of being present in America and contributing to its culture. For example, Danny Thomas (born Amos Muzyad Yakhoob Kairouz) is renowned for his innovations in television sitcom and, more important, for his drawing on his Christian Orthodox heritage to found St. Jude Children's Research Hospital. Fazlur R. Khan was the principal engineer for Chicago's famed Willis Tower, ushering in innovations in structural techniques that sustained skyscrapers. Both were Arab immigrants whose talents propelled them to notice. Neither was a representative of their faith, but both drew on their faiths in their crafts.

The infamous and horrific events of September 11, 2001, changed the lives of many Arab Americans. America declared a war on terror, instituted the USA Patriot Act, and attacked Iraq rather than the lands of the attackers. The lives of Arab Americans were put under extreme surveillance, and thousands were detained, deported, or renditioned (sent to a foreign country that permits torture for questioning). Families were terrorized—children at schools and adults in many workplaces. Arab families were forced to seek assistance from the very agencies that were causing their grief. The war on terror became a war against Muslims and Islam, with Arab Americans sitting in the middle.

The following chapters attempt to both reconstitute the roots of Arabs in America in their diversity and tell the story of their continued presence. This is both an exciting journey through 20th-century history and a tale of not yet resolved conflict.

Acknowledgments

I would be remiss if I did not thank my wonderfully patient and attentive editor, Kim Kennedy-White. Also, I would like to thank ABC-CLIO for the opportunity to really study a community of people here in the United States who contribute and suffer much.

Chronology of Key Dates in Arab American History

1528

The first documented Arab arrives in North America, a Moroccan slave named Zammouri, later known as Estebanico.

1787

The Moroccan-American Treaty of Friendship (Treaty of Marrakesh) is signed, opening trade relations. Morocco becomes the first country to recognize the newly independent United States.

1790

The United States adopts a series of acts that establish a uniform rule for naturalization by setting the residency requirement at two years and requiring the renunciation of former allegiances before citizenship can be granted.

1795

A more stringent naturalization act is passed that includes a five-year residency and the renunciation of former allegiances as well as titles of nobility.

1866

The American University of Beirut is established by U.S. missionaries in the Arab world.

1875

Immigration excludes prostitutes and alien convicts.

1876

The Philadelphia Centennial Exposition attracts a number of businesspeople and merchants from Arab countries such as Algeria, Egypt, Lebanon, Morocco, Syria, and Tunisia.

1880

The Great Migration sees an estimated 20 million people immigrate to the United States from around the world. Some 95,000–100,000 come from Arab countries, most of them from Lebanon and Syria.

1882

Immigration bars the entry of convicts, lunatics, and idiots and those liable to become a public charge, along with any and all Chinese.

1890

Arab churches are established in New York City.

1891

The Immigration Act adds new categories of exclusion that mirror concerns about the biological inferiority of immigrants, targeting those suffering from contagious diseases (such as trachoma, which Syrians seem to carry in large numbers) and aliens convicted of crimes involving moral turpitude (conduct considered contrary to community standards such as polygyny). Immigrants (except for the wealthy) now need medical inspections upon arrival.

1892

The first Arab-language newspaper, *KawKab Amrika* (Star of America), begins publication.

The first federal immigration station at Ellis Island opens.

1893

The Chicago Exposition attracts a number of businesspeople and merchants from Arab countries such as Algeria, Egypt, Lebanon, Morocco, Syria, and Tunisia.

1899

Syrian is added as a classification in the U.S. Bureau of Immigration.

1907

The number of Arab American newspapers reaches 21.

1911

Ameen Rihani's book *The Book of Khaled* is published. It is the first Arab American novel.

1912

The *Titanic* sinks while crossing the Atlantic with 154 Arabs on board; 29 survive.

The Bread and Roses Strike takes place in textile mills in Lawrence, Massachusetts, leading to industry improvements.

1917

The first of a decades-long series of movies from Hollywood portraying Arabs with stereotypes begins with *The Tragedy of the Desert*.

1918
The Friends School in Ramallah, Palestine, is founded by Quakers.

1920
The Pen League establishes a community of Arab American poets, scholars, and writers.

1923
The first Arab mosque in America opens in Highland Park, Michigan.

Kahlil Gibran publishes *The Prophet.*

1924
The Immigration Act of 1924, also known as the Johnson-Reed Act, limits immigrants from each Arab country to a quota of 100 per country per year.

Some 200,000 Arabs now live in the United States.

1930
The number of Arab American newspapers increases to 50.

1931
The Southern Federation of Syrian Lebanese American Clubs is established and includes local clubs in 13 southern states.

1936
The Midwest Federation of American Syrian-Lebanese Clubs is established and comprises several regional clubs.

1936–1937
Arab American Petey Sarron wins the world featherweight championship.

1948
The State of Israel is established in Palestine.

1950s
The second wave of Arabs immigrating to the United States begins and includes a high number of educated professionals, including those from upper-middle- and upper-class backgrounds and English and French speakers from Egypt, Iraq, Jordan, Lebanon, Palestine, and Syria. More Arab students, particularly from Bahrain, Oman, Qatar, Saudi Arabia, and the United Arab Emirates, come to the United States to study.

1953
Congress passes the Refugee Relief Act, allowing increasing quota for Palestinians.

1963
The Islamic Society of North America is founded.

1965
The Immigration Act of 1965 is passed, removing quotas based on country of origin.

1968

The Association of Arab-American University Graduates is established; it is the first Arab American organization.

1970s

The third wave of Arabs immigrating to the United States begins. Many of these immigrants come from war-torn countries and arrive highly educated and skilled. More than 400,000 Arab immigrants arrive between 1965 and 1992.

1971

Arab American William Peter Blatty writes *The Exorcist*.

The Islamic Circle of North America is founded.

1972

The Arab Community Center for Economic and Social Services is established.

1973

The National Association of Arab Americans forms to encourage participation in civic life.

1975

The National Arab American Medical Association is established.

1980

The American-Arab Anti-Discrimination Committee is founded by U.S. senator James Abourezk.

1984

Arab American Doug Flutie of the San Diego Chargers wins the Heisman Trophy.

1985

James Zogby establishes the Arab American Institute, which focuses on civil and political engagement.

1986

Arab American Bobby Rahal wins the Indy 500.

1991

A U.S.-led military coalition launches the Persian Gulf War to remove invading Iraqi forces from Kuwait.

1994

Council on American-Islamic Relations is founded to handle civil and criminal cases of discrimination against Arabs and Muslims.

The first Festival of the Arts (Mahrajan Al-Fan) takes place in New York City; the Arab American cultural event also takes place in 1995, 1996, and 1998.

1996

Ralph Nader makes his first of four bids for the presidency of the United States.

Congress passes the Illegal Immigration Reform and Immigrant Responsibility Act along with the Anti-Terrorism and Effective Death Penalty Act. These acts are most strongly pursued against Arabs and Arab Americans.

The Federal Aviation Administration institutes a profiling system.

1997
The Arabic Musical Retreat is founded and takes place every summer at Mount Holyoke College.

Arab American writer Naomi Shihab Nye publishes the award-winning young adult novel *Habibi*.

2000
The Union of Arab Student Associations is formed.

2001
On September 11, 19 terrorists from Arab countries commandeer four U.S. commercial airlines, attacking the World Trade Center with two planes and the Pentagon with another. A fourth plane crashes in rural Pennsylvania.

The U.S. Patriot Act passes.

The U.S. Transportation Security Administration is established to identify passengers on planes in U.S. airports.

The Arab American Family Services is founded.

2002
The National Security Entry-Exit Registration system is implemented to monitor aliens from Muslim and Arab countries plus North Korea upon arrival and departure. The U.S. Department of Justice conducts interviews and background checks of thousands of Arabs and Muslims.

2004
Zaha Hadid becomes the first woman to win the prestigious Prtizker Architecture Prize.

2005
The Arab American National Museum, the first museum in the United States devoted to Arab American history and culture (and still in 2018 the only such museum), opens in Dearborn, Michigan.

2017
U.S. president Donald Trump signs an executive order banning entry of Arabs and Muslims from seven Arab countries. Litigation over revisions continues.

2018
More than 4 million Arab Americans live in the United States, mostly in major urban areas.

CHAPTER ONE

How Americans Learned about the Arab World, 1600–1900

The earliest Arab immigrants to America came to a world that already had an impression of them based on the product of European upbringing, where tales of adventure and intrigue often had the Arab world as its subject because it was exotic, wealthy, and at a distance.

Some of the earliest American knowledge of the Arab world began with encounters with the Ottoman (Muslim) Empire and thus with Muslims rather than with Arab Christians. Other sources of American understandings about Arabs came from the Europeans who settled America, who had a history of contact with the Muslim world since the beginnings of Islam in the seventh century with the Christian Byzantine Empire.

These early encounters of Europeans with Arab Muslims were rooted in nearly four centuries of trade by land and sea. Religious conflicts were often violent, and the negative sentiments were long-lasting. These sentiments crossed the Atlantic with Europeans who settled America and persisted in thoughts about the Arab world as a place of treachery, thievery, and general barbarism.

The story of strictly American perceptions of the Arab world is seated in an era characterized by rivalry of royal authorities—the Europeans, the Ottomans, and the rising authority of Protestants still tainted by their European experience of Islam and Muslims. American identity building is thus a multifaceted story of political intrigue, religious conflict, and cultural identity building. Needless to say, the drama that unfolded between Muslims and Christians has only been surpassed by the equally compelling story of the building of a nation founded on religious pluralism. The

A shop in the Grand Bazaar, Istanbul. Istanbul is located in the heart of the Ottoman Empire. (Library of Congress)

issues surrounding advocating religious pluralism yet facing the possible
existence of world traditions that were antithetical to a Protestant establishment were complex, and the arguments were intense. The concerns of
religious pluralism have occupied the courts since the 17th century and
persist today.

By the early 17th century, the world was in what we would describe today
as global conflict. A newly emerging Europe found itself encroached upon by
the Ottoman Empire. Almost simultaneously, various European states were
testing the waters for colonialism, with the Arab Muslim world as one target.
The already present internal conflicts caused by the rise of Protestantism
and the wars between nations (the Anglo-Spanish War and insurgent nationalism) made each state wary of its vulnerabilities; at the same time, nascent
efforts at industrialization and national growth pressed the argument for
colonization of other lands with needed resources. Muslims from North
Africa and territories beyond moved into Europe through Spain and southern France, mostly as merchants but also as occupiers in Southern Europe.
Muslims had been governors of what is known today as Spain, Portugal, and
southern France; resistance to Muslim rule resulted in the Christian Reconquista (711–1492), which killed Muslims and Jews who did not convert to

Christianity. The Reconquista violence and forced conversions caused animosities that remained in the memories of many who became invaders of the New World.

Because Arabs' writings of their encounters with Europeans were largely in Arabic and Persian, most of what we know about early Arab history is from the works of European writers. For example, the works of bards such as *Le chanson de Roland* morphed from songs about Basque treachery in the 8th century, and the death of Roland (a national hero) morphed into a saga of Muslim/Christian enmity in the 12th and 13th centuries. The holy war version of the poem dates to the time when the Crusades were just beginning to be launched, and thus the final version portrays the duty of the ideal knight as serving not only the king of France but also the Catholic Church in its battle against Muslims, especially in the Holy Land. The peoples of various European states memorized this history, and it was retold for generations in Europe and later in America.

The Colonial Era

The first few decades of the 17th century witnessed major global changes in European economies, religion, and technologies. By 1630, the European presence in the Islamic world was largely based on trade. Dutch, French, English, and Portuguese merchants first arrived in the late 15th century, attracted by the wealth that could be acquired in exporting luxury items to European markets. Some Muslim governments that desired trading partners to stimulate their own economy encouraged such trade. The Ottoman Empire initially was more isolated because it had a strong internal trade network, but it later expanded this network in trading agreements beginning with France. However, merchants in the Ottoman Empire, Christian and Muslim, began to witness a change in their fortunes as the modern era changed economies and power bases because of new warfare technologies.

Simultaneously, the Protestant Reformation at the beginning of the 16th century affected the religious and political life of Europe. Martin Luther's reformation of Catholic thought opened the door for the rise of Protestantism and the violent upheaval across Europe that followed. The competition for royal authority emerged with the English Puritan revolution, which removed King Charles and executed him while attempting to establish a Puritan commonwealth. During these years and continuing into 1648, the Thirty Years' War raged across Central Europe, bringing destruction as Protestants and Catholics vied for power. At the same time England began to establish colonies in North America, many of them with the purpose of venture capitalism and of spreading one or the other of various interpretations of Protestant Christianity. Biblical Christian governments were established, as seen in Jamestown in 1607, New England in 1620, and the Massachusetts Bay colony established by Puritans in 1630. The King James Version of the Bible, which was released in 1611, shaped the English language and influenced political, social, and philosophical thought in the New World. Ideas for scientific inventions, technologies, and understanding of the universe, which the Catholic Church persecuted in Europe, could and did flourish in the New World.

While many Catholics in Europe focused on the absolute necessity of driving the Ottomans out of the Holy Land, almost all New World Protestants had millennial yearnings. Millennialism is the belief expressed in the biblical book of Revelation to Apostle John (the last book of the New Testament) and says that Christ will establish a 1,000-year reign of the saints on Earth before the Last Judgment. At the end of time, God will judge the living and the resurrected dead through ultimate divine justice. Millennialism was, however, primarily interpreted as a concern with the earthly nature of the New World and thus predicted an overthrow of existing seats of power (which at that time meant Britain's and France's hold in the new land). An imminent fall of Islam became a rallying point in the series of events heralding the return of Christ. Because of their apocalyptic narratives, early Anglo-American Protestants were drawn into the global plays of power. Islam had always been understood as a serious theological challenge to Christianity. Extemporaneous biblical commentaries by Protestant ministers continued the hostilities in their portrayals of the heresy called Islam that existed in that barbaric world.

All of this political and religious intrigue was further complicated by the presence of Deist statesmen of the new America. Deism (a belief in God but disenchantment with organized religion and notions of the Trinity and biblical inerrancy) arose as a theological position during the Enlightenment in England, France, and Germany. Adherents wanted a restraint on religious control of government but understood its moral necessity as a component of government.

The diversity of the faiths among the 55 delegates to the 1787 Constitutional Convention demonstrates the broad intellectual and theological thought and values that went into the writing of the foundational documents of the United States. There were 28 Anglicans (Church of England, called the Episcopal Church in the United States), 21 Protestants of various communities, 2 Roman Catholics, and 4 anticlerical participants who debated over the nature of governance of the new land. They also brought with them to this convention perceptions of potential relationships to the rest of the world. Many of the founding fathers held slaves and participated in providing the biblical and political rationale for slavery and the genocide of native populations as they sought freedom from tyranny themselves. The tales of Arab Muslim lands dominated the theological thinking of many when it came to world religions.

Early Experiences with the Arab World

Though trade was still conducted in Muslim lands, medieval representations of Islam (though not Orthodox Christianity) included tales of the beliefs promulgated by a false prophet of a false religion who was licentious and whose people were barbarously indoctrinated in "vileness" in the name of the religion of Islam. Captain John Smith, whom most readers know from his engagement with the Indian woman named Pocahontas, began his career as a military man in Europe in wars against the Ottomans. He became quite a legend fighting Ottoman Turks in Europe before coming to the colonies. Smith considered himself a "hearty crusader against the Muslims" (Mar 2006, 2). *The True Times,* one of the first secular autobiographies published in the West, describes how Smith vanquished three Turkish warriors by dueling in 1602. He was granted a coat of arms portraying three Turks' heads. His coat of arms appears in the corner of one of the earliest maps of old Virginia and has the motto "to conquer is to live." Near the end of his time while battling the Ottomans, Smith was captured and sold to a Muslim woman, thereby rendering him into slavery. Finding that Smith was uneducated, the Muslim woman sent him to her brother to be trained; he escaped and was later free to encounter Pocahontas in the colonies.

On this stage and with the actors somewhat in place, European and thus early American perceptions of Islam and Muslims were both accurate and ill-informed. The Ottoman Empire was most times despotic and allowed few if any rights to its subjects even if they were Muslim; cruelty was imposed on non-Muslims. It is equally true, however, that the Ottoman rulers were far more interested in the taxes they could extract from the various parts of the empire than the welfare (or lack thereof) of its subjects. They treated their empire much like the Holy Roman Empire had treated its subjects before its demise. While Europeans are asserted to have abhorred the excesses of the Ottoman Empire, they engaged in the same sorts of excesses in their own empires, inaugurated with colonialism and later with U.S. imperialism using invasion and subjugation. The restriction and abolition of rights seems to go hand in hand with the creation of empires. The combination of the political with the religious is not new but has been enhanced in the modern era and heightened as the rhetoric of rivalry by both Arab and Western countries increases and expands. Arab Christians found themselves caught in the middle of the rivalry, as they were Christians who, living in the Arab world, were thought to have been tainted by Islam because they spoke and read Arabic.

Arab Christians nevertheless suffered under taxes, land confiscation, and general second- or third-class citizenship. Arab Muslims who did not serve as managers or provincial administrators suffered because they were Arab and not Turkish. Nevertheless, the theological, ideological, and political problems persisted in the entire Mediterranean even though Christians and Muslims lived side by side.

Islam as a religious tradition and worldview has been contested by the Christian world since its inception and since the division of the church into its Roman Catholic and Orthodox branches. The theological problem is Islam's denial of the divinity of Jesus, along with the denouncement of how Christian devotees came to proclaim him as God rather than as a prophet and messenger. This led to charges that Islam is a false religion whose adherents committed unspeakable acts of violence to spread the religion. Nevertheless, Ottoman attempts at religious tolerance were notable for being a bit better than what existed elsewhere in other empires, such as that of Spain. Of course, there were lapses in everyday tolerance by governors and their administrators, leading to excesses between established policy and its actual practical application.

Protestant Christians faced a new challenge at the beginning of the 17th century with their national prescription of religious freedom for all. Did that include Muslims, Jews, Catholics, and Orthodox Christians? If the Ottoman Empire was barbaric because of its imperial rule, then what was the Catholic Church that they wanted desperately to renounce? What happens to religious freedom in that mix?

These debates followed the settlers to the New World, as questions of religious freedom were a core aspect of identity for the new nation. Many of the debates on how to form the new republic refer to the European perceptions of Islam and Muslims as an unwanted challenge to the values of the Protestant New World but a theoretical model of Muslim governance in Spain if there was to be an inclusion of Jews and Catholics. Orthodox Christians are never mentioned. Theory, however, turned to reality with the exploits of the new nation and the Barbary Wars.

The Barbary Wars and the United States

The Barbary States were a collection of North African territories, many of which practiced officially supported piracy in order to exact tribute

The U.S. Navy bombards Tripoli in 1804 during the Barbary Wars. (Library of Congress)

from weaker Atlantic and Mediterranean powers. Morocco (though an independent kingdom) joined Algiers, Tunis, and Tripoli in a loose allegiance to the Ottoman Empire for trading purposes. The United States fought two separate wars with Tripoli (1801–1805) and Algiers (1815–1816). At other times the United States preferred to pay tributes to obtain the release of captives held by the Barbary States, mostly because it did not yet have a national navy.

The practice of state-supported piracy and ransoming of captives was not unusual in the 17th- and 18th-century world of trade on the seas. Many European states committed horrors in attacking each other's ships, all while participating in the transatlantic slave trade. The two major European powers, Great Britain and France, found it expedient to encourage the Barbary States' policy of piracy and paid tribute to them, as this allowed their merchant shipping industry an increased share of the Mediterranean trade. Barbary leaders had chosen in turn not to challenge the superior reach of the French navies.

Prior to independence, American colonists had enjoyed the protection of the British Royal Navy. Timothy Marr asserts that "Africa symbolized to Americans a compound of political tyranny and anti-Christian darkness, a potent mixture that lent credence to the view that inhabitants of Barbary were truly barbarians" (2006, 27). Even the geography of the Barbary Coast, which consisted of a narrow coastal region harboring a huge unexplored continent with mythical deserted interiors, stroked imaginations of monstrous semihuman inhabitants or at least peoples whose alien religiosity, dark skin, and purported lack of civilization produced rationales for their enslavement. However, once the United States declared its independence, British diplomats were quick to inform the Barbary States that U.S. ships were open to attack. Clearly this was a move to test the power of the newest player in the game of rivalry of royal authorities.

This permission to attack led to the capture of several American citizens by the 1780s. By the 18th century debates over slavery had commenced in the United States, yet statesmen did not see any similarities between American slavery and the enslavement of American citizens in the Barbary States. Nevertheless, America began to win over the Barbary States when it was able to form a federal navy. Encounters continued, however, mostly with Protestant Christian missionaries, travelers, and adventurers to the Middle East.

American Protestant Christian Missionaries to the Arab World and Back Home

The perceptions of the Muslim world perpetrated by missionaries were undoubtedly created from Protestant church teachings, commentaries, and tracts produced about the Muslim world by Europeans and expanded by the personal experiences of missionaries. It is important to note, however, that there is a difference in Protestant encounters: early missions (early 19th century) to the Muslim world, then known as the Ottoman world, were conducted by Protestant evangelicals; later missions (later 19th century and early 20th century) were conducted by mainline Protestants. The missionaries' beliefs about themselves and their missions are important to comment on here.

Evangelical Protestants believed that their faith carried an imperative for universalizing evangelization. From this point of view, they looked with disdain on other religions including Islam, Judaism, Roman Catholicism, and Eastern Orthodox Christianity. Socially and culturally, these missionaries saw their faith as one, which often required the rejection of previous loyalties, traditions, and orthodoxies. Evangelical Protestants joined churches they liked rather basing their religious choices on family tradition and loyalty, and thus their religious culture became highly individualistic. Needless to say, these efforts found little correspondence with Arab families and individuals in the Ottoman world but did have other effects.

Those initial encounters in 1819 acted as the second contact, though this time intentional, between the United States and the Muslim world. Evangelical Protestants used the tracts written by some of those who participated in the Barbary Wars (18th–19th centuries) as a map to the pagans, Mohammadans, and "dead" Christians, meaning Orthodox Arab Christians. They added to already formed perceptions of Muslims as violent and anti-Christian.

The perspectives of mainline Protestants were to prove extremely devastating for Arab Muslims and frustrating for Orthodox Christians. Mainline Protestants, following in the wake of evangelical Protestants, first continued the mission of attempting to convert the heathens and "dead" Christians. What they heard in response, rather than a welcome for Christian salvation, was a plea for assistance in building primary and high schools and technical schools and colleges. Though done under the scrutiny of the Ottoman administration, these missionaries did what they could do with their resources, establishing the Syrian Protestant College in Beirut (which would become the American University of Beirut in 1920) and the American College for Girls in Istanbul. The learning of English in these schools made its graduates great candidates for American citizenship. Nevertheless resentment did begin to grow, as the missionary schools became outposts for American political propaganda. What the missionaries brought back home laid the foundation for an ignorance of Orthodox Christianity and a demonizing of Islam.

Little was said about Orthodox Christians beyond the fact that they had been culturally tainted by Islam and needed saving. Muslims, however, were cast as barbaric and heathen because of their anti-Christian religion; past antipathy between Islam and Christianity; their membership in the tyrannical, oppressive Ottoman Empire; and their participation in the Barbary Wars. The brutal American Revolution resulted in a hatred for despotism of all kinds and gave birth to a perpetual fear of its return. The Ottoman Empire was the newest study in tyranny until its collapse, practically at the end of World War I and officially in 1924. Despite the fact that the subjects of the Ottoman Empire had no say in its administration, initial Arab successes in the Barbary Wars led to representations of them as inhumane and tyrannical with extreme sexual appetites. This did not change despite the eventual success and termination of hostilities by the United States.

Founders such as Thomas Jefferson found some aspects of Islamic thought useful, while founders such as Benjamin Franklin (who had been kidnapped during the Barbary Wars) found everything about Islam abhorrent. Muslim ascendancy in the Mediterranean was a challenge for a new United States that wished to spread its brand of democracy and Christian values to the world. Scholars assert that this is the probable beginning of American political thought about spreading political and religious influence. Remarkably, the Arab disdain for the Turks was almost equal in degree to that of the Americans. American conflation of Arabs with Turks, even if they were under Turkish rule, is quite astonishing given that missionaries would have heard a great deal of the angst from Arabs about Turks on their visits; another agenda was in the making.

Religious pamphlets, caricatures, and literature lay a foundation for civil society that remains today. With Muslim ambassadors in the early 19th century appearing from time to time in the United States along with prisoners from the Barbary Wars, some Americans did have the opportunity to actually see the subjects of their scorn; yet their presence only put a face on the barbarians they had seen in plays and read about in pamphlets and books.

The world of Islam harbored illusions of wealth and beauty in the presence of gold embellishments on furniture and veiled women while hiding a devilish religion practiced by cunning, dishonest, violent people. Visitors to Muslim lands in the 19th century had observed some men in turbans and robes along with shy women covered in colorful nonrevealing clothing. These images were real. They were, however, made sinister. Simultaneously, Christian religious writers depicted the prophet of Islam as part beast and condemned him to the lower regions of Hell. Muslim schools were indeed minimalistic, and methods of discipline were very stern. The method of study was rote memorization with a rocking motion, similar to that of Judaic study. Most visitors had never seen this approach and deemed it and the discipline of students barbaric. Nuggets of truth were given a new narrative, and hyperbole transformed perceptions into stereotypes.

Profiles

Al-Zammouri (?–1539) is considered the first Arabic speaker to arrive on the shores of North America. Born in Morocco, he was captured and sold into slavery, likely by the Portuguese, and renamed Estebanico. Around 1511 after spending more than 16 years in captivity, he joined a Spanish expeditionary force in Florida. He was able to escape after a shipwreck in the Gulf of Mexico. Between 1528 and 1536, Zammouri traveled more than 6,000 miles and is known for his exploration of the U.S. Southwest. In 1539 he was killed by Zunis in present-day New Mexico. The artist John Houser created a statue honoring him that stands in El Paso, Texas.

Pliny Fisk (1792–1825) became one of the first U.S. missionaries in the Middle East. He was one of eight siblings born into a poor farming family in western Massachusetts. His intellectual abilities enabled him to attend Middlebury College and then Andover Theological Seminary, where he trained to become a Congregational minister. It was a time of religious revival in America when his denomination along with other mainline churches insisted that the clergy should be educated. In 1810 the Congregational Church founded the American Board of Commissioners for Foreign Missions, the nation's first major missionary organization. Fisk was sent to the Middle East.

References

Ameri, Anan, and Holly Arida. *Daily Life of Arab Americans in the 21st Century.* Santa Barbara, CA: Greenwood, 2012.

Heyrman, Christine Leigh. *American Apostles: When Evangelicals Entered the World of Islam.* New York: Hill and Wang, 2015.

Marr, Timothy. *The Cultural Roots of American Islamicism.* Cambridge: Cambridge University Press, 2006.

Naff, Alixa. *Becoming American: The Early Arab Immigrant Experience.* Carbondale: Southern Illinois University Press, 1985.

CHAPTER TWO

Beginning to Settle or Not?

1890–1930

How Arabs settled in the United States is very much a story of when they settled and the shadows cast by the vagaries of conflict in their former homelands. It is similarly a story of the U.S. history of national formation, cultural imagination, and immigration. The specific story of Arabs, however, is one of a diverse religious and largely homogeneous linguistic group of various nationalities, the majority of whom are Orthodox Christians. Since the largest group of Arabs to come to America prior to World War I was Christian, the story begins there.

Prior to World War I: Old Life

Arab American Christians are descended from ancient Arab Christian clans such as the Melkites, Maronites, and Rum Eastern Orthodox Christians who did not transition to Islam and settled in Transjordan and Syria. Arab Christians also belong to the Greek Orthodox and Latin Churches in Syria and Palestine. On the whole, Arab Christians came to America from Egypt, Iraq, Israel, Jordan, Lebanon, Palestine, North Africa, and the Arabian Peninsula starting in the 19th century and continuing through the mid-20th century. Living in predominantly Muslim lands primarily as largely autonomous religious groups brought them all under Ottoman Muslim rule at the beginning of the 14th century.

Under Ottoman rule, Arab Christians were protected and enjoyed a limited amount of religious freedom. While they were free to worship in their churches, they could not build new ones and had to get permission

Arab immigrants in New York City in the early 20th century. (Library of Congress)

to repair those that had stood for centuries. They were also subjected to paying an obligatory tax for non-Muslims under Islamic law, requiring a community leader who was responsible for collecting these taxes and then paying the local authorities. Many left the lands of their birth due to a combination of forces, including significantly higher Ottoman taxes, second-class citizenship, and the changing economic fortunes in the Middle East due to the opening of the Suez Canal in 1869. Whatever the specific reasons, Arab Christians came to America in noticeable but not significant numbers when compared to other immigrants from Europe in the late 19th century; initially, only a few families or individuals were Muslim. A short review of history will make the need for immigration clearer.

The economy of Lebanon and the surrounding areas of Transjordan, Palestine, and so on suffered two major economic crises in the mid-1880s. The first was the opening, under French control in 1869, of the Suez Canal, which connected the Mediterranean Sea with the Red Sea. The canal changed the economies of the Middle East by becoming the major route for goods coming in from Europe and the Far East. The impact was devastating for some Middle Eastern products, such as silk. Now consumers in Europe had choices of the kind of silk used in luxury goods and paid lower prices by getting goods from Japan. Consequently, the demand for Middle Eastern silk shrank, causing some of the farms to lose revenue and owners to seek other means of employment and income. The 1890s also witnessed devastation to grape farms caused by microscopic lice that demolished crops without remission for years. These two major economic disasters propelled as many men out of the region as could escape to find economic promise. The United States was one destination.

Many of these men were poor, uneducated or undereducated, and unskilled in the trades needed in the United States. They had been owners or managers of farms, not involved in the industries that were building in the United States. Like other immigrants to the United States, they saw themselves as temporary residents with hopes of making significant amounts of money to return home, buy land, and support families after the economic woes disappeared.

Landed

In the United States, Arab farmers found themselves confronted again with daunting odds: isolation from family and the familiarity of home, loneliness, and a need to cultivate a different grade of land with different and harsher weather conditions. Most were unsuccessful in farming and turned to an equally grueling form of manual labor: peddling. The peddling of carpets, housewares, pottery, spices, and fabrics was not quite as profitable as a successful farm but was a distinctive alternative to failed farm initiatives. This work produced money from each sale rather than waiting for a payment from a farm crop that may or may not produce. This enabled the most successful peddlers to realize the dream of constant work with the ability to quickly amass money to save and send home. Additionally, peddling did not require training, extensive capital, or extensive knowledge of English. Peddlers could sell what they brought from the homeland and whatever relatives could bring.

Peddling strengthened character and introduced Arab Americans to their neighbors in new ways. It required the development of thick skins in the face of those who ridiculed peddlers' poor language skills and their appearance. They endured verbal abuse from children and disgruntled customers, who often thought that because of language deficiency on the part of the peddler they could be cheated in the sale. Peddlers subsequently did not live psychologically stable lives even when their financial security was not destitute. Psychological stability was secondary to the larger goal of returning to the homeland.

Since most of these immigrants were men, they kept their contacts within all-male Arabic-language groups in clubs and bars and lived in tenements (sometimes sharing rooms), forming a sort of Arab male ghetto. There was no initial interest in long-term investment such as buying land, homes, or businesses. Generally, women were brought from home for marriage with the expectation that families would return with money to settle in the homeland. The idea of resettling in the homeland became complicated by British and French colonization, however.

No Return

The upheaval in Middle Eastern economic, social, and religious life caused by colonization was significant around the globe. For many Arab Americans, this situation severely limited their contact with home along with the ability to send money and find brides.

British forces occupied Iraq, Jordan, and Palestine, while France reorganized and colonized Syria and Lebanon. Although many in the population welcomed these colonizers as liberators from the Ottomans, the relief was short-lived and was ultimately resisted. Colonization changed much in literature and poetry, basic staples of societal standards of beauty, history, and values. Arabs inserted new standards of beauty, racial coloring, and body morphology. Simultaneously, the flow of financial assistance from peddlers and small businessmen almost ceased, and communities were reorganized under new rule. Despite the British, French, and Russian rule, in the United States "Ottoman" remained the listed category of origin of many Arabs until the Treaty of Versailles (1919), which declared that former Ottoman countries were independent states. Meanwhile, the United States began to legislate its first policies on immigration in 1897 with an urgent need to attract more Europeans and limit numbers of people from other lands.

The Arab world of the 19th century did not know representative democracy or citizenship. Much of this world was suffering under various colonizations—French, British, Italian, and Ottoman. There were monarchies and military rulers. Christians, Jews, and Muslims lived, intermarried, and suffered together. Colonization was designed to conquer peoples and render them subjects. Europeans began to colonize while the Middle East was still under Ottoman control and after the demise of the Ottoman Empire began the process of building a different type of society.

For some Middle Easterners, colonization was not such a bad thing during the 17th, 18th, and 19th centuries. This was especially true for minority religious communities. In Lebanon, for example, Maronite Christians found a defender in the French, just as the Druze found a supporter in the British. European merchants increased the amount of trade in an effort to make their bids for control, all the while bringing new technologies into the region and thus changing the social and economic landscape.

The British and the French, of course, were not quite fair in trade or the dispersal of access to technology. While some families saw an increase in their wealth and thus their stature, European merchants and advisers benefitted the most. The presence of colonizers created more religious tension, as they instituted their own laws. As the Muslim majority ruled in those countries, Christians fell under even more persecution than they had under Ottoman rule. Stiffer taxation and limited ability to expand their communities made migration a tempting opportunity, which many took advantage of.

Immigration Laws Prior to World War I

Initial immigration acts regulated and welcomed immigration from the European world to help further build the population of the United States as an outpost of Europe for the religiously disgruntled and those ready to seize opportunities that only unsettled lands could bring. Most of the immigrants were Europeans who were Christian and generally shared those ideals and values. The composition of the groups entering the United States began to change in the 1830s. Substantial groups of Irish and German Catholics came to a country that was overwhelmingly Protestant Christian with no love for those under the pope's authority. Yet economic needs, reinforced by the ideals of opportunity and freedom, were more deeply rooted in the country than was the anti-Catholic heritage or fears of foreign takeovers. During the 1890s, immigration patterns again changed as the new immigrants appeared to be more "foreign" than the old ones.

"Alien" characteristics were what many older Americans saw—strange physiques, coloring, customs, and languages. The new immigrants were often disliked and feared. Some were East European, while others were from the Middle East. They were considered culturally different and incapable of understanding the U.S. version of self-government, and because they belonged to the inferior races of the Ottoman Empire and other locations, they were thought to be biologically and inherently inferior as well. European and American researchers had begun to classify the world's population by grouping racial and geographical characteristics, ranking them in order of superior and inferior intellectual development.

Racial categories, as evolved by Johann Friedrich Blumenbach in 1775, listed five major racial divisions: Caucasoid, Mongoloid, Ethiopian (Negroid), American Indian, and Malayan. Though Blumenbach did not arrange these divisions in a hierarchy, the racial theories of founders such as Thomas Jefferson were influential, placing Caucasians (Aryan heritage) at the top and blacks (African heritage) at the bottom.

In the 1880s shortly before Arabs began a significant immigration to the United States, the United States passed its first racist, restrictionist law, the Chinese Exclusion Act. Americans on the West Coast protested that their declining wages and economic ills were because of Chinese laborers, although the Chinese population only constituted .002 percent of the total population. Congress passed the act to placate worker demands and to comfort concerns about the maintenance of "white racial purity." This act suspended Chinese immigration for 10 years and declared the Chinese to be ineligible for naturalization. Chinese immigrants already in the country tried unsuccessfully to challenge this act. The act was renewed in 1892 for another 10 years, and in 1902 Chinese immigration was made permanently illegal but then was modified for a small quota of individuals primarily from Taiwan and Hong Kong when those regions declared autonomy from mainland China in the 1950s.

The need for Chinese labor that had been welcomed to lay railway lines and work in mining was at an end. The success of the restrictions on Chinese immigration led to more direct restrictions in immigration as nativists realized that their voices had power. One of those nativist moments came in the form of pleas for literacy tests, which effectively also stymied the right to vote for blacks though it was designed to obstruct unwanted immigrants. Immigrants with little or no knowledge of English were treated harshly. Nativists loudly protested the arrival of nonwhite immigrants and Arabs, leading to some Arabs claiming an Aryan heritage (though they could not pass literacy tests). This situation was even more remarkable in that at the time, masses of white citizens would not have been able to pass these literacy tests either.

Settling on an Identity in a Racialized Country

Citizenship is a universal and distinctive feature of the modern political landscape of Western nations. Every modern state formally defines its citizenry, publicly identifying a set of persons as its members. The rights and privileges of citizenship by Western countries are in stark contrast to those countries where there are rulers and subjects rather than representative governments and citizens with rights. Subjects served the governments of distant lands at the arbitrary will of occupying armies.

Colonial subjects functioned under laws foreign to their cultures and their moral values. In most instances, they were forced into illegal (and many times immoral) acts to survive. Colonial powers also formed managerial classes from among their subjects to inform on dissenters and to keep the masses under control. Many in this managerial class sacrificed their own cultural identity to adopt the cultural identity and bearing of a foreign power. They were hated by the masses because they lived at the behest of the oppressors, many times with wealth. When the winds began to carry odors of revolution, many in the managerial class agitated to become the new rulers on behalf of the colonialists. Others in this class escaped to the lands of the colonists or to the new world of the Americans with as much wealth as they could transport, leaving behind productive enterprises that would maintain their wealth. They traveled, however, with some from those masses whom they had formerly oppressed. Some of the Arabs who came to America landed as members of the managerial and merchant classes and as such were relatively privileged, with first-class accommodations on steamships.

Early Americans truly thought of themselves as builders of a new world. They were clear that they did not want to be European, although they sought to expand upon and exceed European notions of industry and invention. Newly established Protestant Christian communities were determined to create their own version of Christian practice while simultaneously seeking freedom from religious persecution in Europe. Freedom was interpreted as being able to function by communal consensus and being free from rule primarily by the Catholic Church or a monarch. They could own land and build whatever they wanted. Although many early colonialists still felt that religion must play a role in governance for morality's sake, the establishment of courts quickly reflected the diversity of religious interpretation present.

Even though many colonialists were relatively poor, they did not want the destitute, ex-prisoners, prostitutes, or sick whom they believed would cripple the moral fiber of the new land and strain the resources of the new society. Moreover, they wanted white Protestant thinkers, inventors, entrepreneurs, and families to build a nation. The yellow, brown, and black races of the world could be indentured servants or slaves to work on the project of building America, but they were not to be included in its benefits. Christian Arabs had to prove that they were Christian and sometimes had to prove that they were white to benefit. Muslim Arabs had to prove that they were worthy.

As previously stated, since Arab immigrants came from the Ottoman Empire, they were all branded Turks or Ottomans and subjected to all the stereotypes that being called a Turk engendered both culturally and religiously. Ironically, Syria did not exist as an independent nation at this time; only local inhabitants and government authorities described the area stretching from the Taurus Mountains in the north to the Sinai Peninsula in the south as "Syria." When the Ottoman Empire fell at the end of World War I, they all received a new name—Syrian and then (after Lebanon as created by the Europeans) Syrian-Lebanese. Syrians, however, were categorized as Asians though they "looked" more white than Asian.

Arab immigrants, especially Syrians, sought to be categorized as white, which had much more to do with American racial policies for citizenship than any inherent racial animus on the part of Arabs at this time. Whiteness became a pragmatic utility.

Racial identity is one of the primary means by which immigrants assimilate to the United States. All immigrants are placed into a racial hierarchy, which becomes the fundamental means of establishing an American identity. These categories are negotiable to an extent. Though Arab immigration to the United States began when Arabs accompanied Spanish explorers to the region in the 15th century, this is not common knowledge. One of the first Arabs in the Americas may have been Moroccan slave Al-Zammouri (also known as Estebanico), brought in 1528. During the American Revolutionary War horses exported from Algeria replenished the American cavalry, and Morocco was the first country to officially recognize the independence of the United States in 1787 in what is known as the Moroccan-American Treaty of Friendship (Treaty of Marrakesh). Yet whiteness, not friendship, prevailed.

Because the United States used whiteness as a precondition for citizenship into the 20th century, those immigrants who came under these conditions adapted their identities to the circumstances. Citizenship was the goal, and because it came with rights and privileges, its acquisition was of ultimate importance for Arab Americans.

By December 1909, a young Syrian immigrant who had fulfilled all the requirements for citizenship except either whiteness or African descent was denied citizenship. After raising the money necessary to get a lawyer to argue his "whiteness" and Caucasian ancestry in court, only then was he granted citizenship; his skin color was white as opposed to brown.

Whereas Syrians found themselves mired in sectarian and religious strife at home, in their new home they became racialized, consciously placing themselves within America's racial hierarchy, causing further psychological strife. While researchers have questioned why this small minority of immigrants is so widely represented in the legal literature in cases of racial discrimination, this research poses some possible answers. A great many were phenotypically different from the dark caricatures of the Turkish (Arab) horde imagined in the literature of the day, and early

Americans had little knowledge of the genealogical charts of those living in the Arab world. Thus, phenotype went a long way in proving "whiteness." But this was not the only measure even for those who were deemed white. Other measures included skills potential or already possessed wealth. Possession of skills such as barber, carpenter, or shoemaker or money on hand was proof of their ability to perform "whiteness."

The fight to prove "whiteness" of immigrants divided itself in the same ways as the sources of racial categories. A. H. Keane's *The World's People* categorized the people of the world into four classes—Negro or black, Mongol or yellow, Amerind, and Caucasian. The geography covered by the Caucasian class included the territories of "Syrias," and thus some judges used this to certify Syrians as white and therefore eligible for naturalization. Other judges emphasized the importance of being of European descent, those who from tradition, teaching, and environment would be predisposed toward the U.S. form of government and living. The unfortunate presence of trachoma (a bacterial disease that if left untreated causes blindness) in a significant number of Syrian immigrants was further evidence for many judges that these immigrants could wind up in the same indigent population as "coloreds" and potentially among those angry and disenfranchised such as blacks in the South and those who had recently migrated to the North.

What was underlying these questions of "whiteness" and proposals of literacy tests? It seems as though the general feeling was that the new immigration was dominated by the so-called inferior peoples—those who were physically, linguistically, and mentally different and therefore less desirable than the native-born or early immigrant groups. Ex-slaves were still considered unqualified for citizenship on a number of grounds, including the assertion that they belonged to an inferior race. Yet this was not the only impediment for Arabs. What about religion?

Religious Settlement: Unexpected Resistance

Protestant Christians fought to make and keep America Protestant. The influx of often wealthy Roman Catholics to the United States during the first half of the 19th century caused an uproar, since with the families came bishops and then dioceses and canon law. Predominantly Catholic communities began to incorporate property held by Catholics since the 18th century. The responses were quick. Legal incorporations were superseded by the New York state Act for the Incorporation of Religious Societies (1813), with empowerment of trustees who could take into their possession and custody many if not all of the holdings of Catholic communities.

This refusal to acknowledge the canonical responsibilities of the bishop to protect church property called attention once more to the "antidemocratic" nature of the Roman Catholic hierarchy, which reaffirmed the need to attempt to exclude Catholics. Needless to say, those religious communities that followed stood no chance of having any authority that contravened that of the U.S. government.

Between 1870 and 1920 more Catholics and Jews, along with a small but noticeable number of Orthodox Christians, would change the religious landscape. First, Orthodox Christianity had emerged from a small mission in Alaska when the liturgy was conducted abroad a ship harbored in Alaskan coastal waters in 1741. For the next 100 years, Russian Orthodox Christians evangelized among the indigenous populations there. Skirmishes with the U.S. government led some of these Orthodox Christians to move to the East Coast and later, along with immigrants from the Middle East, Orthodox Christianity became one of the fastest-growing religions in North America at the time. In 1890 these new immigrants, distinguished by religion from Protestants from Northern Europe, entered the United States in noticeable numbers. Despite initially being labeled illiterate, unskilled, and other slanderous terms, Eastern Orthodox Christians became some of the wealthiest Christians in the United States. Needless to say, they were still not welcomed and quickly became invisible. Beginning in 1909, the number of restrictions on entrance and naturalization began to increase.

For the very few Muslims and Jews present, however, the ongoing tension from claims that the United States was a Christian nation (despite efforts of the founders to separate church and state) posed myriad problems. Public schools had been open since the middle of the 17th century in Massachusetts and used the Bible as a text for learning to read. Witnesses were sworn into court proceedings first using the New Testament only, which left Jews unable to be sworn into court proceedings, and then the Old and New Testaments, which caused protests from Quakers and others who thought that one should never take an oath on the Bible. And as with other Americans such as some Protestant sects and atheists who refused to swear on the Bible, Muslims found their civic participation compromised by the Protestant ethos of the land. Supreme Court justices, such as the famed Joseph Story, argued to ensure that religion, specifically Protestant Christianity, remained a part of the public order in commentaries on the U.S. Constitution. For all other religious communities, this meant a privileged position for Protestant Christianity.

Nevertheless, small ethnic Orthodox Arab communities established a religious presence as early as 1906, such as Cleveland's St. Elias Church. In Chicago, St. John the Baptist Melkite Church was established in 1910, and the Syrian-Lebanese Syrian Club of Chicago was established in 1918. In 1915, St. Maron (Maronite Catholic) was established in Detroit, Michigan. As with most immigrant communities, differences in worship and membership in particular religious lineages emerged as soon as enough people and money permitted separate churches. There were not enough Arab Muslims in Cleveland to form a community large enough to establish a place of worship until 1960.

Arabs also established a number of small social organizations to assist with assimilation and socialization of new immigrants in Cleveland and Chicago. They created Arabic-language radio shows and newspapers to keep them informed about Arabs in America and the Middle East. The Syrian Ladies Society of New York was founded in 1907, and the Southern Federation of Syrian Lebanese American Clubs was founded in 1931. As early as 1930, they held annual festivals where they could gather as a language group for a short period of time. As with other late immigrant religious communities, as soon as enough followers of one rite (set of sacraments) came, they founded churches of their own.

Once an initial group of settlers came together, they created a chain migration along ethnic and religious lines. Religious communities were established, and subsequent family and religious supporters joined them.

Public schools and the courtroom became the essential places of learning civics for Americans and thus how to participate in the public sphere. The United States was plural in several ways at its onset, but a relatively consistent civic base was required of all citizens. Lessons focused on the rights and duties of citizenship. Young citizens learned about voting, some basics of taxation, jury duty, and the branches of local and federal government. In the courtroom, citizens were expected to know their rights and be responsible for their duties. Also taught in addition to civics lessons were history, reading, writing, basic science, and arithmetic; American students learned little about the rest of the world except for those countries that had direct contact with America.

The fact that the first nation to recognize the sovereignty of the United States was a Muslim nation was not in the nation's textbooks, nor were accurate accounts of settler encounters with indigenous populations. The history of slavery was briefly referred to as a needed intervention in the affairs of a heathen people. Immigrants were supposed to observe and then practice the etiquettes of America, and where their homeland manners differed, they were to ascribe the American way as a priority. The privileging of Protestant Christianity was put into effect at the outset and continues to be a subtle though persistent message in classrooms, courtrooms, and public spaces. Protestant Christianity won the information war.

This state of affairs happens in every society; visitors and those seeking longer-term residencies are expected to acclimate to the general rules of behavior and the laws of that country. This does not prevent immigrants from practicing their religion or even their understandings of values in their homes unless it goes against the law. It is often stated that ignorance of the law is not an excuse for breaking the law.

American Wars and Arab Americans

Arab Americans, though rarely referenced, are veterans of wars from the American Revolution to the present. For some, this was a ready path to citizenship. In 1924, Princeton professor Philip Hitti found that 13,965 Arab Americans had served in World War I; most were from Greater Syria. Subsequent researchers assumed that Hitti's numbers were accurate and claimed that this group was the largest number of ethnics serving in World War I. While this is certainly not true, as at least 350,000 African Americans served, the attempt to demonstrate the willingness of Arab Americans to serve their new country is a point noted. According to Hitti's research, by World War II an even higher number of Syrians had served than any other ethnic group, again untrue but a noted demonstration of their patriotism. More recent scholars have since culled military records and found that around 15,000 Arab Americans actually served. The National WWII Museum in New Orleans lists over 1.2 million African Americans as veterans, though they were segregated at home; perhaps this is why Hitti did not list them. Nevertheless, the military was one place where an American identity and heritage began to be established for young Arab men in the first half of the 20th century.

While World War I was indeed a watershed event in the psyche of those Arab Americans who continued to envision returning with wealth to the homeland, other global and local politics continued to dominate their conversations in the United States. The quotas set after World War I, which restricted immigration from the Middle East to 100 per year no matter what country, served to increase feelings of isolation among those already settled. The quota system made it risky for Arabs to return home, since they might not be allowed to come back, and many lost their dreams of bringing relatives and/or brides to the United States.

Though the immigration system matured somewhat after World War I, it became even more wary of "aliens," continuing to introduce quotas to balance the numbers of European migrants with those coming from the Asian Arab world to their pre-1800 levels. Fear of potential deportation as "undesirables" caused Syrians to embrace assimilation; for many this meant changing their names, not teaching their children Arabic, and not having pride in any heritage other than their American one.

Arab immigrants to America coped with the shock of difference and struggle with accommodations of values and work in America. Their first-generation children (born in America) had little knowledge of the ancestral home beyond the stories and pictures from their parents. Name changes and the choice to not speak Arabic at home only further estranged them from relatives back home and those in America who had not learned English. Arabic-only community newspapers had to become bilingual to engage younger readers and to keep relevant. The hopes, fears, and aspirations along with the necessary accommodations, acclimations, and challenges are only now being acknowledged as states document their immigrant past.

Alongside and in spite of a history of attempts at exclusion, many Arab immigrants assimilated easily into American society. Facilitated by Anglicization of Arab names, few Americans in the general population distinguished them beyond their preferences for certain foods, manners, and speech. Since children were not taught Arabic and since the lack of an ability to return to the homeland decreased its attraction, Arab immigrants increased their use and mastery of English, leading a few to become well-known authors. Simultaneously, all Americans were living in a nation that was quickly changing its global and national identity regarding industrialization and technology.

America's focus on becoming a world power after the demise of the Ottomans and European powers, along with great losses of over 400,000 able-bodied men at the end of World War II, fueled a need for workers despite the quota system. Those immigrants already present saw discrimination and competition over jobs but also high employment in infrastructure placement. The surge to become the world's only superpower took the focus off Arab immigrants and temporarily put it on Jews fleeing the Nazis. The land of the free decided at the time that it did not want to assist in that rescue of Jews until American Jews and the rest of the world made that position untenable.

Nevertheless, for Arabs until after the creation of the State of Israel there was a momentary sigh of relief regarding their own immigration woes. Communities began to settle. In the 1980s, Palestinian Arabs (Christian and Muslim) began arriving in the United States in a steady though still limited number. They replenished the financial lines from the United States to Palestine, boosting the economy and the social lives of the people there. They also used chain migration to bring relatives into the United States for citizenship. The increase in numbers over the last 30 years has made Palestinian Arabs the largest group of Arabs in the

United States. Communities settled into small enclaves in urban and suburban spaces across the country.

Community Newspapers

For many Americans, newspapers played a significant role in shaping the life, cultural concerns, political opinions, and history of communities. For Arab Christian and Muslim Americans, newspapers were also a way to communicate the news from and to the old homeland. These newspapers connected "little Syrias" and "little Palestines" in New York and Michigan to communities across the country and to Mount Lebanon in the Middle East.

Many papers were established within a few years of arrival. In 1898, Naoum Anthony Mokarzel in Philadelphia founded *Al-Hoda* (The Guidance) as the first Arabic newspaper in the United States. Mokarzel had been a well-known opposition writer who fled Mount Lebanon. In 1903, he moved the newspaper (original location unknown) to Little Syria in New York. This eight-page newspaper was written in Arabic without translation. Ideologically, *Al-Hoda* supported the French in their bid to occupy Syria and Lebanon in the aftermath of the Ottoman demise. In 1899, *Meraat-Ul Bharb* (Mirror of the West) was sold in communities in New York and beyond. It was founded by Najeeb Diab, also Lebanese from the same region. Diab too was a critic of the Ottomans and especially their treatment of Arab Christians. A series of newspapers followed—*As-Sayeh* (The Pilgrim, 1912), *Al Bayan* (The Explanation, 1910), and *As Sameer* (The Entertainer, 1926), which demonstrated the prowess of Arab intellectuals among the immigrants. These men sought not only to keep readers informed of the conflicts at home but also to interpret the new world of the Middle East for them. They encouraged readers to learn English so they could play a role in American political life.

Other Industries Pre—World War I

Though much existing research has led to a few extraordinary stories of the lives of Syrian and Lebanese immigrants and issues of identity and belonging, little has been said of some of the skills and industry they brought to the United States. One such industry was textile production.

Assy Shaheen arrived in the United States in 1887 and within a year opened a dry goods store. A decade later, the next generation arrived from Lebanon and opened a manufacturing plant and clothing store in Manhattan, producing mainly women's clothing. These workers were more likely

A silk factory in New Jersey, 1914. Arabs established this industry in the late 1800s. (Library of Congress)

to be Arab Christians who toiled as weavers; they brought a long history of silk weaving from Lebanon. They already knew how to own and operate the machinery needed to produce luxury items, which at the turn of the century were in high demand. Moving some manufacturing from New York to New Jersey, they made Paterson, New Jersey, the "Silk City" of the United States. Remarkably, there is little information on this transfer of vital skills.

The work of Arab women was critical; as weavers, they could provide supplemental income to support families, send money to the old homeland, and assist in bringing family members over to the new land. Of course, the wide-scale employment of women had its downside—unmarried women were earning a living and mingling with men, for instance. Evidence in reports shows that churches denounced these women, and such critiques were reported in Arabic newspapers. Whether this was an attempt to thwart women's potential independence is not corroborated, but the reporting did in fact stem the rising tide of women's work outside the home. It seems more likely that there was an increasing alarm at the need to protect unmarried women from gossip and strange men in the new land.

Augmenting these skills were the works of poets, writers, and artists. Although this group was small in number, their work indicates that not all immigrants were uneducated. Perhaps the most famous of the group was Khalil Gibran (1883–1931), whose major work, *The Prophet,* is still referenced in literature classes today. The Pen League, a literary circle, was situated in the United States but had its greatest impact in Arab countries as it attempted to analyze what was happening during the demise of the Ottoman Empire and the new incursions of European states. This is a critical note. Arabs, both Christian and Muslim, took quick advantage of their distance from the homeland to weigh in on the political and economic activities there. Some Christians, such as Maronite Christians, advocated for the French occupation of Lebanon, while others sought British rule. Their articles in newspapers also fought the stereotypes in other American media—cartoon caricatures in the *New York Times* and the visuals portrayed in a new industry, American cinema.

American cinema began its depictions of the Arab world beginning in 1921 with *The Sheik,* starring Rudolph Valentino. Hollywood embarked on presenting visual stereotypes of the Arab world in which the men were licentious, thieving, lying brutes and its women were conniving seductresses with alluring veils.

First there was the landscape—deserts, unrelenting blowing sand, and tents. No evidence of civilization was present, as there are no streets with sidewalks, houses, businesses, or factories. Women were scantily clad with abdomens exposed but with sheer veils over their faces—at once appealing and hidden. The men were dressed in robes with white or colorful fabric wrapped around their heads. These men were in search of women, and when white women were introduced as missionaries, adventurers, or just visitors, they became the obsession. Arab men were brutal, often violently kidnapping women and forcing them into submission.

The Interwar Years

Even Thomas Edison made a short film in 1897 in which Arab women were portrayed as seductive, readily available, and easy to include in sexual fantasies. Nonetheless, the interwar years were filled with plenty of visuals of the world the immigrants came from. *The Sheik* gave rise to *The Thief of Bagdad* (1924), *A Café in Cairo* (1924), and *The Son of the Sheik* (1926). It is important to note that these films portrayed several different opinions on what was happening in the Arab world globally.

As the British and the French were at odds over who was going to have the upper hand in colonization of Ottoman lands, their fights and the civilization that the West represented were depicted everywhere in these movies via military dress, stereotyped Western mannerisms, and cultural references. The impression given was that European women were free to travel the world and sometimes to participate in the affairs of state, remaining feminine and innocent. European women were sold as slaves by European-educated Arabs who could not resist their "nature" to treat women in a degraded manner or extract revenge for unrequited love. French troops were evident in these sandy dwellings, and their presence was shown as natural. These were lands of war, not peace. The people were driven by base instincts such as sex, brutality, and revenge—not the gentility of women and educated European men. U.S. statesmen were clearly cast in a particular light in the global conflicts, which left America as the only safe democratic republic not involved with the heathen Arabs.

Conclusion

As Arabs were beginning to settle as Americans, newer Arab immigrants faced limiting immigration quotas, which prevented immigration of more family members and seriously curtailed their ability to move between the old homeland and the new. America itself was in the middle of a mini social revolution. Women suffrage movements were finally successful in getting the vote in 1920; prosperity abounded as interest in farming decreased and interest and investment in business rose. Tariffs, enacted beginning in 1922, kept foreign goods out and domestic production safe. Throughout the 1920s, private business received substantial incentives. For newcomers, America did indeed appear to be a paradise of sorts.

Restrictions on foreign immigration during the 1920s reflected a significant change in the social environment in the United States. Immigration had risen considerably in the late 19th century and peaked in the early 20th century. Between 1900 and 1915, for example, more than 13 million people came to the United States, mostly Jewish or Catholic with a small number of Orthodox Christians. The alarm of this "intrusion" on the predominantly North European Protestant rule of America was palpable. Some if not many of the older immigrants resented the fact that newcomers were willing to take low-paying jobs without complaint, but more important they saw in the ways of the newcomers from Southern Europe a return to the mores and means of livelihood they sought to leave behind.

As a result of this immigrant surge at the end of the 19th century, nativist appeals intensified. A reorganized Ku Klux Klan (KKK) emerged in 1915 calling for "100 percent Americanism." Unlike the KKK of the Reconstruction era, the new KKK restricted its membership to native-born white Protestants and campaigned against Jews, Catholics, and immigrants as well as blacks. By redefining its enemies, the KKK and its supporters broadened its appeal to parts of the North and Midwest, and for a time its membership swelled from 1915 to the mid-1920s to, researchers say, 1.4 million members.

A series of measures codified anti-immigration sentiment, culminating in the Immigration Act of 1924 (also known as the Johnson-Reed Act), which was modified in 1929. Specifically this act established a quota system that limited immigration from Southern and Eastern Europe (Jews and Slavs) while allowing significant immigration from Northern and Western Europe. These laws limited the annual number of immigrants to 150,000, to be distributed among peoples of various nationalities in proportion to the number of their compatriots already in the United States in 1920. One result of these restrictions was to reduce the appeal of the United States as a desired destination. The Great Depression of the 1930s also caused a sharp drop in immigration.

Clearly, the nascent settlement of Arabs in America had its challenges regarding a change in cultural landscape, language, and potential earnings. Most Arabs saw the need to quickly get as many family members as possible through the naturalization process. Initially, naturalization took only three years of residency and employment of some kind. This process facilitated a small but steady influx of predominantly Orthodox Christian Arabs. Any old religious strife between Christians and Muslims did not disappear, but the trauma of settlement in the new land pushed it into the background.

Significant numbers of Orthodox Christians quickly learned the perception of their faith from both evangelical and mainline Protestant missionaries to their homeland. As part of the civilizing and converting mission of Protestants to the Arab world, they built schools that taught English and in some instances trades that Americans were familiar with, enabling the young people to migrate to America. After reaching American shores, a significant number began reconciling to the Orthodox faith of their families, while others converted to Roman Catholicism rather than Protestantism. Many Muslims followed this path also, converting to either Protestantism or Roman Catholicism especially in Louisiana. Changing religious ties and names put many on the road to becoming American without shackles to old views of Islam or the Ottoman world.

Major industrial cities spawned their own cultures that included all the vices that accompany an emphasis on making money—moral decay, alcoholism, and prostitution. Many in both the urban and rural areas wanted a return to decency. The Prohibition era gained support, especially from churches. The caution of a potential degradation of morality also was heard by immigrants from the Middle East and Southern Europe. Immigrant populations additionally found themselves in the midst of the Great Migration of blacks from the South to the North, bringing more competition especially for factory jobs. Arab settlers became a part of the American landscape but not without the intrigue of a changing social environment.

Leaving behind families and all that is familiar is an awesome task regardless of the era in which it occurs. Even if one has learned some of the host country's language in school, the feeling of foreignness is exacerbated by dialects, humor, or nuances. Urban America of the late 19th and early 20th centuries was dirty and crowded with tenements, with an extremely diverse collection of ethnic immigrants speaking a host of foreign languages trying to make their way. In old places such as the Ottoman world, the largest tensions revolved around the Ottomans as foreign occupiers and also religion. In the new world, the legal inscription of race and color codes were the foundation of civil life. Arab Christians and Muslims learned quickly that their religion mattered, but religion mattered less than their skin color. Both groups had to contend with thoughts of bringing darker-skinned relatives with "old ways" to the new land.

The potential of darker-skinned relatives in the budding era of Jim Crow for the black population surely created much angst in these immigrant households, especially in the South. Southern political leaders mounted strenuous arguments against immigration from the Middle East, as this was thought to be the beginning of the creation of a class who would join blacks in protest against Jim Crow laws.

Simultaneous with the fear of relatives bringing old cultural habits, escalating strife at home and the need to earn money both to survive and to send home made settling difficult at best. Some returned to the Arab world. For others, an adventure to escape the strife in the Middle East became a new adventure in the United States.

Profiles

Najeeb Diab (1870–1936) was born in the village of Roumieh, Mount Lebanon, in August 1870 and migrated to the United States in 1893. Initially he wrote for *Kawkab America,* the first Arabic-language newspaper in the United States. By 1898 he was managing editor of the paper and simultaneously founded the newspaper *Meraat ul Gharb.* This newspaper was dedicated to defining the issues and current positions of Arab nationalism and quickly became known both nationally and internationally. As an ardent activist for Arab independence from the Ottoman Empire, he was on the Ottoman list of dissidents and was sentenced to death in absentia in 1902. Diab advocated for semiautonomous status for Greater Syria in the Ottoman Empire at the Arab Congress of 1913 in Paris as a founding member. He was also an advocate of the Arab literary circles.

Khalil Gibran (1883–1931), born into a poor Maronite Catholic family from Mount Lebanon, learned the Bible and the Arabic language from neighborhood priests. He immigrated to the United States in 1895 with his siblings, where his birth name, Jubran Khalil Jubran, was changed to Khalil Gibran. His mother, demanding that he learn about his heritage, sent him back to Beirut just three years later to study in a Maronite prep school; he continued in a higher education institute there before returning to the United States almost a decade later. Although best known for his literary works, Gibran was also an accomplished artist in pen and ink drawings and watercolor.

Assy Shaheen (?–?) arrived in the United States from Lebanon in 1887 and opened a dry goods store in 1888. By 1898, the dry goods store expanded to include manufacturing and clothing in the Syrian quarter of Lower Manhattan. Shaheen and Sons opened in 1920 and was a renowned business with a large manufacturing plant in the center of the garment district in New York City, including a silk mill. Shaheen's son Alfred became a textile industrialist who popularized the Hawaiian shirt.

References

The Arabs: Who They Are, Who They Are Not. 1991; release, Films Media Group, 2013.

Gibran, Khalil. *The Prophet.* New York: Knopf, 1923.

Jamal, Amaney, and Nadine Naber, eds. *Race and Arab Americans before and after 9/11: From Invisible Citizens to Visible Subjects.* Syracuse, NY: Syracuse University Press, 2008.

CHAPTER THREE

Arab Culture in America

Previous chapters have explored various aspects of the history of Arab Americans, who have become prominent in the news especially since the horrific events of September 11, 2011. The U.S. government, in the form of utterances from President George W. Bush, claimed that there were simmering hatreds for the freedoms and security employed by U.S. citizens. Though these claims were not specific, evidence of that hatred lay in the ruins of lives and property in New York City as well as Arlington, Virginia, and rural Pennsylvania. Questions quickly emerged about Arab culture and its compatibility with an ever-evolving American culture. This chapter explores the basic foundation of Arab culture and its challenges with American cultural understandings.

Cultural Belonging

Arab culture is patriarchal. Patriarchal cultures prioritize the rights and dominance of males privately and publicly and include, to a limited extent, older women, who have a say in family decision making. Gender roles aid in the maintenance and perpetuation of patriarchy. Males inherit most of the assets of families and are given priority in education, financial management, relationships, and determining family values.

Along with being patriarchal, Arab communities are what scholars call collectivist. In collectivist societies, people define and understand themselves as members of a social group rather than as autonomous individuals. Career and marriage choices are made in consultation with the family rather than based on an individual's desires, skills, or aptitude unless the family is persuaded. Family needs are determined by males; professional

Due to racial violence and profiling, Muslim Americans participate in a candle-light vigil in Detroit. (Jeff Kowalsky/AFP/Getty Images)

skill level, financial status, and general prestige in the larger community are weighed when considering potential male spouses, while domesticity and family status are considered for potential female spouses. The educational system in many parts of the Arab world is structured to assist those from wealthy and middle-class families in getting good educations in private schools rather than merit-based education. Poorer families struggle to pay the school fees for supplies and uniforms required for their children to attend free schools, which are by all reports inferior. Families also tend to be large with five to seven children, regardless of financial level, to maximize efforts to obtain males who can acquire skill sets to either lift or maintain family status. Arab communities have extreme difficulty with female-led households even if the situation results from the death of a male head of household. Female-headed households set a dangerous precedent that could lead to individual autonomy.

Women in most if not all Arab countries cannot rent apartments or lease villas to live on their own without male supervision; otherwise, they encroach upon the honor and integrity of the family. These women would inspire suspicion about their comings and goings along with their chastity, undermining the cultural values of not only the family but also the society.

Arab cultures developed along tribal systems, as opposed to an integrated system of unrelated individuals. Families are the centers of any power in communities, as they set the values and dispense rewards and punishments for disobedience. Families additionally are the safety nets. Children are expected to remain at home until married, though they may return home in times of financial stress or the death of a breadwinner. Children are taught to rely only on family for social, financial, and even practical decisions. Maintenance of family honor and cohesiveness are paramount.

Each family member is charged with a collective responsibility for the behavior and demeanor of each other family member. This includes upholding the family honor, a constellation of behaviors whose primary holders are females. Since the actions of an individual reflect not just on that person alone but also on the entire family, the most gullible and venerable, and thus most susceptible to tarnishing the honor, are females. Young women are expected to use marriage to enhance the family's status and fortunes while young enough to bear many children and should not be set in their ways or too educated. Family reputation (and thus access to education, employment, and respect in the community) is always on the line. Any breach such as unregulated (outside of marriage) sexual conduct is potentially catastrophic. But the ingredients of family honor do not end with appropriate gender behavior; they include generosity, honesty to each other, and (for males) courage and bravery.

Social Political Life

In the 20th century, much of this family structure was challenged by the violence at the end of the Ottoman Empire, the trade route built through the Suez Canal, pestilence, and European colonialism in the region. Arabs were challenged but not broken because of centuries-old family traditions of interdependence. Physically and psychologically, families grew to include extended family in financial affairs, including responsibility for school fees, housing costs, marriage, care of the elderly, and business concerns. While these adaptations were organic, they had a down side in that the family still did not begin the integration processes necessary for the social, financial, and potential issues evolving on the modern global scene. Holding onto values became an obsession, and again, women became the focal point of maintaining traditional culture. Control over women's bodies and the spaces that they occupied were as important as religious ideology.

Ethnic pride, family values, and efforts to control ideologies such as Western imperialism and occupations brought despair. Patrilineal kin groups grew as families reorganized themselves after the fall of the Ottoman Empire. Men in the father's group formed businesses where they could make family corporation-type entities, moved families close to each other, and controlled the family finances. Families simultaneously became culturally even more isolated as Arabness fractured along national lines. Syrians touted their uniqueness from Egyptians, Jordanians, and Lebanese. While some of this ethnic distinction is the result of European powers redrawing the map of what was now known as the Middle East, occupants began their own nationalist moorings. Though there are no differences in basic culture and values and only minimal differences in cuisine, national politics and closeness of alliances with Western states strained liaisons with other Arabs. Mimicry of Western ideals of democracy and secularism (socialism and/or communism) were also distinguishing marks.

Women's social life through all of the societal changes was restricted to the family. Their dress—in veils and *abaya* or *jalabah* (long cloaks)— was considered modest and traditional. Any deviation was considered an affront to family honor. Restrictions on women's movements also restricted their abilities to get education and employment.

A New Reality

Disparities in wealth, access to education, and access to Western norms largely determined who even envisioned the arduous journey westward. The very top tiers of wealth certainly saw few advantages in immigrating to new lands beyond establishing their businesses. Some of their children, however, had been Westernized by attending Christian schools set up by American Protestant missionaries who assumed that Arab Orthodox Christians would convert to Protestantism upon arrival in the new land. Families who saw opportunities to recoup family status (eroded by pestilence and the fall of the Ottoman Empire) came in small numbers.

Previous quotas on non-European non-Christian immigrants from Greater Syria were not lifted. In the Arab world, family lineage and wealth were the primary distinguishing qualities for admittance and citizenship. Rumors sent back from the few who undertook the journey confirmed that race and religion were dominant factors in America, classifying the population. Thousands of Arab Christians and only a few hundred Arab Muslims immigrated during the first few decades of the 20th century. Arab identity questions were subsumed under race-based definitions. In the Arab homeland, Muslims were the majority. In America Christians were the majority, but identity by race intervened to separate white

Anglo-Saxon Protestant Christians from Middle Eastern Christians even moreso than religion.

Immigration Policies

Race classification has dominated American immigration policies since the founding of the country. North European Protestant immigrants have always been preferred over others, despite claims to the contrary. This preference is best seen in the challenges presented to citizenship and property holding rights all the way to exclusion, as in the Oriental Exclusion Act, also called the Chinese Exclusion Act, that lasted from 1870 until 1920.

At the turn of the 20th century labor demands increased the need for immigrants, and the first Arab immigrants answered the call. Schools set up by American Protestant Christians in the Arab world touted the advantages of America for Arab Christians who could convert to Protestantism. Orthodox Christians, on the other hand, saw an outlet for their faith. For American authorities they were not European, but they were at least Christian if they could prove it in immigration courts.

Arab immigrants, mostly Christians of the Orthodox branch, sailed into this new world under the presumption that they had opportunities to reestablish family fortunes and explore new frontiers.

Rumors of racial segregation and the preference of Christian religious membership traveled widely in the Middle East and tempered the immigration of Jews and Muslims. There is an almost complete absence of detail on the arrival of Jews of the Middle East to America. It is important to remember that European Jews have always been a part of the American fabric, but those men and women were not Jews from the Middle East. Perhaps this is why they are generally omitted from texts examining Arab Americans.

Jews had lived in what was now being called the Middle East since antiquity and remained in the geographical region throughout Christian and Muslim empires. As second-class citizens, they nevertheless innovated and created within prescribed boundaries to survive and in a limited sense thrive, even as they belonged to the land before either Christians or Muslims. Capitalizing on European hatred of Muslims/Islam and with outreach especially from France, some Arabic-speaking Jews who sought to take advantage of an opportunity to migrate to more prosperous lands moved there, as the United States was considered unwelcoming. Many Jews remained on their land in the Middle East and would do so until the creation of the State of Israel in 1948. Thus, Jews do not figure in any of the legal accounts of Arabic-speaking immigrants and the problems they experienced with the courts in the early 20th century.

Leaving and Arriving

As with all journeys, there is anticipation and a bit of trepidation. Leaving the familiar is difficult, especially if the endpoint of the journey is an unknown, but is also an adventure. It was especially difficult when so few Arabs of any religious tradition were traveling to the United States. Passengers in steerage class probably had one of the most arduous adventures of their lives, as they could only eat what food they had packed and take whatever medicines they could carry, and they protected what money they had by sewing into clothing seams.

Ship manifests are almost impossible to read today; although they are preserved and accessible online, the writing is tiny and worn with age. Most of the ships headed to America began their journey in lands controlled by Europeans. It is assumed that Arabs had to make it to ports on the Mediterranean or along the Suez Canal in order to begin their journey. Once at the port, the wait to board a ship could take days or weeks, consuming medicines, food, and money. Many historians assume that most passengers traveled steerage to save money, but steerage tickets were the majority and were sold without space reservations as an economic advantage to shipping companies. Steerage was the worst part of the ship: tiny deck spaces in the belly of the ship where noisy, dark, and unsanitary conditions were overwhelming. The mortality rate was 10 percent per voyage for all steerage passengers. An immigrant's identity was often reduced to "alien" on the ship's manifest.

American Protestant Christian evangelical associations, whose missionary arms had contact with the Middle East as soon as the Suez Canal opened the Middle East to Europe, served as stateside conduits for the settlement of many Syrian Orthodox Christians. Although Arabs were a tiny fraction (numbering perhaps a few hundred) of the estimated 15 million migrants who entered the United States between 1880 and 1910, their experiences can be deduced from the stories of the larger groups. Ships from around the world brought as many as 6,000 migrants per day into harbors in Boston, Miami, and New Orleans who disembarked from ships that had been at sea for weeks to months. These migrants all had to be transported to Ellis Island for processing.

The Wondrous Ellis Island

President Benjamin Harrison designated Ellis Island as the site of the first federal immigration station in 1890; it opened in 1892. Because it had protected the New York harbor system during the American Civil

Immigrants at Ellis Island receive medical examinations in 1902. (Library of Congress)

War, it had tiers of circular gun turrets and the appearance of a guarded prison or fort, reported as very scary for many children and adults alike. Those migrants who came between 1892 and 1897 would have been interrogated more for their race and political beliefs than anything else. Of course, there was always scrutiny regarding tendencies for vagrancy, prostitution, and profound physical or mental illness, but the opening of the Ellis Island hospital in 1902 amplified those questions. Many researchers have proclaimed this hospital as the world's first truly international public hospital for the diseases of the world.

The Ellis Island hospital became the proving ground for suitability for entrance into the United States; only first-class passengers and those second-class passengers who brought money were assumed to not be carriers of disease or to become burdens on society. Lower-class immigrants had to wait to be carried from their ship to Ellis Island by barge or ferry; once on the ferry, they typically waited for hours without food, water, or protection from inclement weather. Upon arrival, they were exhausted; no doubt some appeared to be lunatics or idiots due to lack of sleep. Arrival at the registry hall required migrants to walk to and then up about

60 steps as the first fitness test. At the top of the steps stood doctors and nurses who could determine by observation obvious lung/heart conditions and orthopedic handicaps.

Arabs found themselves greatly outnumbered by Italians, Germans, Jews, and East Europeans, all speaking their native tongues. At least 20 different languages were common, but translators were only available for the major West European languages (Italian, French, and sometimes German). The processes at Ellis Island were reasonably efficient for the time but were nevertheless gut-wrenching for the migrants. Legal and health inspections often took days if not weeks.

In large rooms, off of an even larger registry room, doctors and nurses positioned themselves behind long tables with basins full of potassium chloride (used as a wide-spectrum disinfectant) to see patients. Patients, presented in large clusters, were told to remove their clothing and were examined in about 6–10 seconds for obvious disease. Those who passed went on to be questioned, while those who did not were marked on their clothing with chalk for further inspection and in many cases for some treatment. This portion of the process was gender segregated except for physicians and was a dehumanizing process irrespective of nationality, especially for women. Children were separated from their parents as they too underwent health inspections. In some cases, if one child was found to have a contagious disease, the mother and any siblings were deported, sometimes leaving the father at Ellis Island with the struggle to both get the child cured and get all of them back to the United States. With one in five receiving a chalk mark, the hospital was always full.

When those who were detained for further medical inspections became well, they had to present themselves before the Board of Special Inquiry, composed of inspectors. Despite all the dehumanizing and anxiety-producing aspects of the process, only about 2 percent were deported; for these, insolvency or incurable disease rendered them unfit for work and thus a potential or real burden on the public.

Ship manifests listed passengers' names and the answers to a few questions that had been asked upon boarding: Why are you going? Do you have family there? How are you going to support yourself? On the Island, however, the questions were more numerous and detailed about destination, means of support, and political beliefs. None of the current scholarship makes mention of questioning about religious beliefs; perhaps it just wasn't asked until the applicants applied for naturalization. After processing through Ellis Island, immigrants who came from specific towns or groups could reorganize again into those same groups and find their cohorts in the increasingly teeming New York City. Women who were pregnant when they arrived at Ellis Island often left with children given foreign names by doctors or nurses that the new mother could not pronounce; many of the adults left with new names, as inspectors could not pronounce their birth names. A new world and a challenging life in the United States awaited them all.

U.S. Immigration Law in Brief

In the original statute of 1790, Congress prescribed that a free, white, male alien who had resided in the United States for 2 years (including residence of 1 year in any state) might be naturalized by any common law court of record, provided the person was of good moral character (attested to by unrelated witnesses) and took an oath to support the Constitution. Five years later the statute was repealed, and new provisions were added; residency requirements were increased to 5 years, and applicants were required to renounce their former allegiance and to swear allegiance to the United States. Popular hysteria against the new "aliens" caused the enactment of the Alien and Sedition Acts and repeal of the more liberal provisions of the 1795 law. Additionally, required residence was increased to 14 years.

By 1905, President Theodore Roosevelt stepped in to provide some oversight and procedure to immigration law. He put administrative supervision over naturalization in the hands of a federal agency but left to the courts the authority to grant or deny citizenship. Applicants were now required to sign the petition for citizenship in their own handwriting and to speak the English language if capable of speech. They also needed at least two character witnesses to testify to their residency and moral uprightness.

Critical to this study of Arab Americans is the fact that common law courts initially had no procedural rules to follow. This enabled judges across the land to use their own criteria to evaluate applicants; in cases involving Arabs, the old criteria of whiteness, language, and the common law understanding of America as preservation of a Christian nation was paramount. When supervision by a federal agency was put in place, examiners could recommend to judges whether or not an applicant was eligible, and many examiners sought to maintain whiteness and membership in a Protestant faith as the standard for admission.

Legal Identity of Arab Americans

In addition to having foreign names imposed, replacing birth names for many immigrants, the ever-changing world of political tides caused changes in their nationalities of origin and further changes in identity. Naming represents continuity of heritage and inheritance. When names are replaced, a part of identity is shattered. Shifting politics overseas and the creation of new nation states produced changes in the national affairs of regions in the former Ottoman Empire; thus, Turks became Arabs and sometimes Syrians and later Lebanese. This is disconcerting when reading the annuals of legal immigration history referring to that group of immigrants.

The Naturalization Act of 1790 made whiteness a prerequisite for American citizenship; the act remained in force for 160 years until it was repealed in 1952. Legal scholars have sifted through the annals of immigration filings to explore the nature of claims, along with the reactions by judges. According to much of the legal literature, judges in common law courts could examine whiteness, religion, and language as prerequisites for naturalization.

In general, Arab, Syrian, or Turkish identity was an automatic disqualifier for citizenship in the United States. The legacy of the Barbary Wars in addition to missionary diaries and reports about travel in the Ottoman Empire had laid the foundational attitudes about Arabic speakers and Islam. All Arabic speakers in the region had been tainted by the corruption of the Ottoman Empire and impressions of the religion and culture of Islam. Judges, either not understanding or ignoring the presence in the Arab world of Jews (since antiquity) and Orthodox Christianity (since the fourth century), demanded proof that Islam and Muslims had not tainted Christian applicants. Nevertheless, approximately 130,000 Arabs applied for citizenship between 1870 and 1930. A challenge to this misperception of Arab identity was taken up in 1906.

In 1906, George Shishim presented himself before Judge George H. Sutton to petition for citizenship in a California superior court. Shishim had lived in California for 25 years, and evidence of his exemplary membership in the community was verified by his service as a police officer. The naturalization examiner held the position that Shishim's Arab identity disqualified him for citizenship and conveyed this to the judge. Shishim testified that he was indeed a Christian from the same region as Jesus. Shishim prevailed and was the first immigrant from the Arab world to be naturalized as an American and judicially ruled white by law. His naturalization, however, did not change the treatment of other Arab immigrants.

Other issues used to deny immigration (such as indigence, illness, or disease) were also applied in the case of Syrians, many of whom had the infectious eye disease trachoma. This disease often results from crowded living conditions and poor sanitation in many urban centers of the Middle East and if left untreated can cause blindness. The prevalence of this disease caused immigration officials to deny admission to those suffering from it on the grounds that it is infectious and renders people unable to work. In response, a number of Syrian immigrants, especially those with trachoma, used brokers to come into the United States through Canada and Mexico, swelling the official numbers of Syrian immigrants during this period.

A Quiet Time

As the world wars took over the public consciousness of the populations of Europe and America, Arab Americans were pressed to demonstrate their patriotism, survive the economic depression, and regroup. Migration to America slowed, and the processes and policies for immigration to America became more standardized and restrictive. Arab Americans settled into a newly imposed (though superficial) identity. With Arab Americans prevented from traveling back to their ancestral homelands, their identity consolidated a pattern of hybrid identity and tenuous belonging. American history makes no substantial mention of Arab Americans organizing on behalf of Christian or Muslim Palestinians.

For this group of immigrants, identity became a looming set of concerns. They were seen as savages following an evil religion or at least being influenced by it. They inherited all of the horrible stereotypes and caricatures of the Ottoman Empire. The fact that their numbers were minuscule among the various groups of immigrants did nothing to remove these factors. The experience of Ellis Island was particularly devastating because many immigrants were renamed, thereby obscuring connections to a previous life. There were explicit and implicit demands to forget their foods and language and many times their religion.

Palestinian Christians and Muslims

The 1948 Arab-Israeli war would again put Arab identity in jeopardy, as the public heard about the appropriation of ancestral lands. This war also catapulted Palestinian Arab identity to the forefront of "Arab identity," supplanting Syrian, the primary Arab nationality, used at the beginning of the 20th century.

Abandonment of family or land in Palestine was not an option, and the long fight to maintain claims began. While many families had sought to assimilate by losing language and accents, language maintenance again became a necessity for travel back to the ancestral land. Indoctrinating youths to the importance of remaining as long as one could on the land and being able to converse with those there became a strategy. Socialization regarding gender roles and other cultural habits formed a mainstay of child rearing.

This strategy, however, worked against full assimilation. Adult Arab Christians maintained much of their religious heritage, though they too had to relearn Arabic and employ the strategy of indoctrination of youths to keep homesteads in their hands as much as possible. Simultaneously and perhaps because of the 1948 Arab-Israeli war that involved a number of Arab Muslim states, Arab ethnicity again and more concretely became synonymous with Muslim and in many instances synonymous with Palestine.

By the time of the First Intifada (1967), a Palestinian revolt against Israeli occupation, many Arab Americans from Palestine and Lebanon, both Christian and Muslim, found themselves sponsoring newly minted refugees from Palestine and Israel. They also found the need to comply with Israeli rules about the necessity of continuous occupancy. The Absentee Property Law was enacted at the creation of the State of Israel to facilitate Jewish acquisition of property. The only way around this law for Palestinians was continuous occupancy. This meant that family members had to return to the homeland themselves or send children to house-sit the property for at least three months. Thus, Arab Americans with land to preserve were American some of the time and Arab for indefinite periods of time. Children's education was disrupted at home and abroad.

Many young Arab Americans of Palestinian descent found themselves living transnational lives without roots. Parents took teenagers and young adults out of school and out of work in the United States to go to Palestine to tend to family property and the elderly for long periods of time. This often meant that children found themselves not promoted in school, while young adults were fired from jobs. These circumstances made continuity in belonging problematic. School friendships were sometimes lost, as were peer relationships in jobs; careers were constantly interrupted. As schools closed for the intifadas in the 1960s and the 1980s, Palestinian youths lost years of schooling overseas, while Arab American youths lost years of schooling in the states, as they often had to assist in keeping occupancy in Palestine. The increased necessity of an Arab identity was coupled with the need to experience what being Arab meant in the homeland. This situation further bifurcated an Arab American identity.

In the United States, this drive to preserve home highlighted difference and alienness, despite longings for Americanness and the privileges of whiteness. Nevertheless, Islam and the Palestinian issue became representative of most Arabs, even those from areas other than Palestine. Before 9/11, the number of Arab Americans from Libya, Morocco, Algeria, and Tunisia paled in comparison to the number of Palestinians, Christian and Muslim. While the majority of Arab immigrants were Christian, the focus settled on Arab Muslim Palestinians. "Arab" in the American mind was conflated with "Muslims" in the media.

Palestinian and Muslim as Hegemonic

Tens of thousands of Arabs from Morocco, Sudan, Somalia, Egypt, and other Arab countries arrived and found themselves put in the mix of negative attitudes. Their national identities were dislocated further by their de facto identification as Palestinian Arab. Some Arabs considered themselves to be cultural Muslims instead of believing Muslims—those born into practicing Muslim families or nonpracticing families living in the Muslim world. The onset of various ideologies in the Middle East (such as socialism, liberalism, and communism) gained adherents in many countries. Consequently, some born in the Middle East were only Muslim culturally. They had distinct grievances against the religious strictures introduced by secular and religious leadership along with the backwardness introduced by colonialism. Coming to America and finding themselves identified as Muslims and identified solely with the Palestinian struggle as opposed to the struggles of their own lands was another dislocation.

The solidification of this identity was seen during the Iran hostage crisis, when many Americans who could not distinguish Iranians from Arabs by phenotype or language began attacking those they thought were Arabs on the streets in major cities. As Israeli evictions of Palestinians from their land continued and increased, the need to identify as Arab increased; however, the identity of Muslim and the integration into America became strained.

As Jewish Americans made the case for Israel and won backing in the U.S. Congress, Arab Americans found themselves beginning to face overt discrimination. A civil rights organization, the Council on American-Islamic Relations, was founded in 1994 to handle the tide of complaints. But now a Muslim American identity became a possibility, ignoring all the diversity, much to the chagrin of many Christian Arabs.

A Major Setback to Any Hope of Assimilation

The tragic events of September 11, 2001, ushered in an identity crisis for Arab Americans, religious and not religious. Even those who looked like the caricatures of Arabs were in danger. When the perpetrators of the attack were identified as Arabs, accounts of mayhem against individual Arabs and their communities increased exponentially. The official numbers of Arabs deported are generally inaccurate, as many were renditioned for torture outside the United States. Many put the figure between 15,000 and 20,000. Some Arabs changed their names, while others attempted invisibility. Many older Arabs had maintained their accents or spoke very little English. The test for almost all Arabs became proving assimilation and integration while maintaining Arab identity in the midst of a national crisis caused by some of their own countrymen.

American news outlets showed pictures of the hijackers and cast wide nets of potential coconspirators, which seemed to include every Arab male age 12–50. Deportations, renditions, and detentions began and still remain a possibility for any Arab American male. Students from elementary to university classrooms documented discriminatory treatment focusing on name and presumed alienness. Classrooms became grounds for bullying, as teachers' and classmates' disparaging comments about Arab heritage became increasingly common across the land. Some teachers' egregious behavior made national news because they were reprimanded or fired. Many older males found themselves not admitted to colleges and universities, being fired from jobs in which they excelled, or not even being invited to an interview. Changing names did not change the phenotype published in newspapers.

After 9/11, the Arab Muslim identity reigned as the seemingly only Arab and Muslim identity, though Arab Muslims continued to be only a fraction of Arab Americans and of American Muslims. Carrying the weight of these given and assumed identities has put the younger generation in identity crises. Many choose nicknames before their teachers and classmates give them one. They assume grafted American personas such as cool, comedic, or trying hard to get along. Others have adopted a resistance stance, whereby they demand to be called by their full names and use every opportunity to demonstrate pride in heritage or religion. These and other identity issues prompted one professor to publish a book titled *How Does It Feel to Be a Problem?*

What Could Have Caused 9/11?

While Arabia is the home of Islam and Arabic is the language of its central text and classical scholarship, the preeminence of Arabs in Islamic thought has been a slowly decreasing claim to centrality in modern times. The response to this set of circumstances has caused a series of other efforts to cement that preeminence. Saudi Arabian scholars sought to spread Wahhabism and its cultural manifestations throughout lands where Muslims lived and make Arabic the only language of Islam. This was an attempt to homogenize the diverse cultures of Islam, which has proven problematic though somewhat successful around the world. Wahhabism as a distinctive ideology of Arabia fit the political and religious situation at the end the 19th century.

Wahhabism "reflects some of the most important trends in eighteenth-century Islamic thought" (DeLong-Bas 2004, 8). In the Middle East, it was one of several reform movements of the time and was sculpted to the context of Arabia. All of the reform movements sought to stop the deterioration of Islam, as they perceived changing thought and practices. All of these reform movements felt that rulers and the people had adopted beliefs and practices into Islam from other religions or even animist practices.

Many of the beliefs and practices were in direct contradiction to the central tenets of Islam—strict monotheism and belief in the prophet of Islam as a messenger of God. The seriousness of the situation and its spread led some thinkers to reeducation programs. In general, there was a call to return to the fundamentals of faith, focusing on beliefs and practices. As scholars have noted, this did not mean violence, militancy, or even literal readings of the Qur'ān, but it did mean a move away from a millennia's worth of historical interpretations that had accrued as Islam spread around the world. Muhammad ibn Wahhab himself promoted a scripturally based practice of Islam that included reading the Qur'ān and making a just society. How his teachings were later interpreted and implemented in Arabian society is quite a stretch. Nonetheless, it served to bring together the disparate practices of Islam that are present on the Arabian Peninsula. While this is a theological/ideological position in what is now Saudi Arabia, its execution around the world where there are differing political environments has proven destructive. The worldwide spread of later Saudi Arabian interpretation spread as the authoritative version of Islam for Muslims everywhere. Muslims from the Middle East brought these notions with them.

Arab Muslims became the resource ethnic group for all things Islamic in America to the exclusion of other ethnic communities of Muslims. Some who came from nonreligious families, both Christian and Muslim, pushed themselves to the forefront of knowledge about Islam. This scenario, of course, has not gone without challenge but remains into the 21st century.

In the 21st century, external and internal acts of terror committed by Muslims of varying ethnicities are still seen as Arab terrorism. Even attacks in revenge are thought of as blows against Arabs. Many first- and second-generation Arab Americans joined interfaith groups or emphasized their Americanness in Muslim newsletters. Some Arab Christians joined in the protests over discrimination.

Arab American identity was concretely set into the mold of Arab American Muslims in the 21st century, with Arab American Christians fully receded into the background. Many Arab American Muslims began to fully identify as Arab first, living in America as citizens. Children continue to be sent back to Arab homelands to be indoctrinated into Arabness, causing conflicts with their American lives. Some Arab American young adults are choosing the American life over the Arab life—until a catastrophe in Syria hits social media and/or the news, causing them to join fund-raising efforts for refugees or travel as medical professionals to assist those in need.

According to researchers, there has been a great shift in the identity of Arab Americans from the margins of the mainstream to its outer boundaries. It is notable to remember the uniqueness of the Arab American experience. Many earlier groups are not affected by the external events and governmental policy toward their home countries. Today the ban against Muslims, but not against Christians, coming from seven countries reflects the continuing "othering" of Arab Americans. It is troubling that this current state of events further complicates Arab Americans' American identity.

The 2016 presidential election further exacerbated the problems of Arabs. Many immigrant Muslims were thought to be Arab or associated somehow with Arabs. Republican presidential candidate Donald Trump stoked the fears of many Americans with rhetoric that demonized America's diversity as he targeted refugees and immigrants, particularly Mexicans and Muslims, as the cause of many of America's ills on the criminal and economic fronts. With slogans such as "make America great again," uttered after telling refugees, immigrants, Mexicans, and Muslims to "get out," it became clear to listeners that in order to make America great again, diversity needed to be extinguished. Mexicans are hunted and deported, while Arabs are surveilled and sometimes deported regardless of citizenship status.

The ban on Muslims coming to the United States from seven Arab-majority countries ordered by the Trump administration to fulfill a campaign promise has wreaked havoc on Arabs, whether Christian or Muslim. Anxiety is high, as there are new attempts to stop chain migrations of parents and relatives.

Conclusion

What was for many centuries an identity based in language, culture, and religion has undergone and continues to undergo many challenges from within and without. Arab culture is a collectivist culture and is patriarchal and paternalistic. Women are generally not decision makers, and that state plays a great role in controlling the lives of women. The families are in hierarchies, with men on top and with children, especially females, on the bottom.

Arabs came to America, where their names were abbreviated or changed to facilitate a new beginning. Most Arabs came during 1890–1920 and formed ethnic communities to preserve their identification with language and culture. The Great Depression ironically probably did the most to seat them in America, as they suffered along with other Americans.

Arab families are tightly knit, with interdependence, honor, trust, and hospitality forming a basis for cohesion. Much pride is taken in names, lineage, and ties to the land. The opportunities and challenges posed by immigration were undeniable, but many of them were unforeseen. Arab Christians thought they were coming to a Christian land that would welcome them as part of the Christian family rather than marginalizing them. Muslims realized that they would be met with religious challenges but felt that the promise of freedom for all regardless of faith tradition would win out over the challenges. Both were wrong in many ways but correct in many others. Arabs have been able to continue family life, build communities, get educations, open businesses, and even work in entertainment, politics, and media.

Profiles

Nihad Awad (n.d.–) was born in Amman New Camo, a Palestinian refugee camp in Amman, Jordan. He studied engineering at the University of Minnesota in the 1990s and worked as the public relations director for the Islamic Association of Palestine. In 1994 Awad joined with others to form the Council on American-Islamic Relations, America's first Muslim civil rights organization. He was honored by the Royal Islamic Strategic Studies Centre in 2009 as one of its 500 most influential Muslims.

George Shishim (1875–1945) was a Syrian immigrant in Los Angeles. His petition to become an American citizen in 1906 caused significant judicial fanfare. Shishim was first denied by the naturalization examiner on the grounds that he was not white. This ruling was later overturned by an eloquent lawyer arguing for Shishim's Aryan heritage. This case signaled the racialization of Syrian immigrants. Shishim's considerable length of employment as a police officer was not enough to attest to his character.

References

Abraham, Sameer Y., and Nabeel Abraham. *Arabs in the New World: Studies on Arab-American Communities.* Detroit: Wayne State University, 1983.

Beydoun, Khaled A. "Between Muslim and White: The Legal Construction of Arab American Identity." *New York University Annual Survey of American Law* 69, no. 1 (2013): 29–76.

DeLong-Bas, Natana J. *Wahhabi Islam.* Oxford: Oxford University Press, 2004.

CHAPTER FOUR

Faith, Beliefs, and Practices in Arab Christian and Muslim Communities in Plural America

Introduction

The largest groups of Arabs to come to America were from a variety of Orthodox rites, including Eastern Orthodox and Eastern Catholicism (Chaldeans, Melkite, and Maronite). There are about 5 million Orthodox (Eastern) Christians in America. Choosing the largest of the communities, Eastern Orthodox, this chapter provides readers with a brief overview of the Orthodox Church. According to scholars, the Orthodox Church, as a branch of Christianity, has put much of its theological work in the hands of bishops and the patriarchs. Arab Muslims came at the end of the 19th century in much smaller numbers and today number around 1.5 million, with the majority arriving after 1965.

Toward that end, we find that interpretation of core beliefs and how they are actually articulated plays an important role in Orthodox understandings. Language, location, and the authority in bishops came to further divide the Orthodox Church. The result was a series of ethnic churches tied together by their bishops and a patriarch.

Church members communed to reconfirm the tenets of faith and their commitment to it. Children were introduced to the faith community by parents and in prayer. Marriages were celebrations of unions of couples with the faith community, but divorce was permitted under certain conditions.

The encouragement of adoption certainly cohered with the tenets of care in the community.

Immigration to the United States was an extension of the various churches with some initial accommodations. Communities found that they had to coalesce in the same place until enough money could be raised and enough people in a particular ethnic group arrived. Historians charted these developments in newspaper accounts.

Smaller numbers of ideologically different Muslims immigrated to the United States and did so with a majority of Shia Muslims from Mount Lebanon. Their differences with Sunni Islam go beyond issues of community guidance, but the Sunni population, though distinctive, is actually smaller. Sunnis too sought to establish communities as soon as practical on America's religious landscape. The Alawis are included in this chapter because of the prominent role they have played in Syrian immigration from the late 20th century through the immigration crisis of the 21st century.

Clearly the differences between the faith communities did not override the ties of ethnic origin, regardless of faith. The consensus-spoken language was Arabic, as were celebrations of cultural norms such as marriage. Other Americans, when they looked at all, probably saw few distinctions.

The Orthodox (Eastern) Church: A Brief History

Most Americans think about Christianity as Protestant Christianity (in many of its 900+ denominations) or as the Roman Catholic Church. Remarkably, Protestants think of themselves as Christians and Catholics think of themselves as Christians, but many in either group do not consider the other Christian. Perhaps this is a testament to how these branches of Christianity have grown so separately. Worship services of all three branches of Christianity can now be viewed on the Internet and broadcast television. Orthodox Christianity, which has had churches in the continental United States for over 100 years, is rarely spoken of in relationship to the events of Christianity and is not well understood.

The Orthodox Church, the faith of 350 million people around the world, is one of the three main Christian groups. It is made up of a number of self-governing churches that either have their own hierarchy of leadership or are self-governing. These churches are largely divided by regions in the ancestral home and thus by ethnicity; laity follow their particular priest and bishop. All of these communities, however, are linked by a common approach to theology, tradition, and worship. Each church has its own geographic title that usually reflects the ethnic and cultural

An Orthodox Christian church in Los Angeles, 2007. (Ken Hively/Los Angeles Times via Getty Images)

traditions of the believers, such as Greek, Syrian, or Russian. The word "orthodox" means "right belief." It is important to note here that not all Orthodox Churches are Eastern Orthodox and not all churches in the Eastern tradition are Orthodox-Eastern churches.

Eastern Orthodox Church

Eastern Orthodox Christians were the majority of Arabs who migrated to the United States in the 20th century. It is sometimes difficult to distinguish them from Roman Catholics since some beliefs are shared, but they are a distinct group of ethnic churches bound by their patriarchs rather than with an allegiance to the pope in Rome.

At the foundation of Orthodox Christian belief beyond God, Jesus Christ, and the Holy Spirit is Psalm 118:26–27: "God has revealed Himself to us." This is proclaimed in Orthodox churches every morning. Orthodox Christians believe that though God reveals himself he has not disclosed his innermost essence, and thus human beings cannot comprehend this aspect of God. The fullness and perfection of God's self-revelation as stated in Psalms is found in his son, Jesus Christ. Interestingly, the first title given to Jesus, "rabbi" (teacher), is one aspect of his being Christ the Messiah. As a divine teacher, Jesus taught by word and deed. Jesus, who is central to Christian belief and is thought of as the word of God in human flesh, was sent into the world to proclaim God and his gospel. Orthodox teachings state the importance of noting that although God's self-revelation in history is through the chosen people of Israel, the revelation, which culminates in the coming of Christ the Messiah, is of primary importance. All genuine strivings of humans after the revelation in the truth that Jesus brought are fulfilled in Christ. Jesus was a rabbi and a natural link between the nascent community that followed him and the older Jewish community to which he belonged. The writings of Saint Paul declared that Christians are no longer under the rule of Mosaic Law, also known as the Law of Moses.

Mosaic Law refers to the Jewish Torah, or the first five books of the Christian Bible. This law was seen as fundamentally different from other legal codes, as transgressions were seen as offenses against God rather than against the society, which had been the understanding before Moses. This put a deeply transcendental face on "bad actions" that had the force and effect of causing the wrath of God. The law was to be the guidance of the people of Israel and consisted of the Ten Commandments, dietary restrictions, and moral laws governing murder, theft, adultery, purity, and sacrifices along with instructions on the upkeep of the Tabernacle.

This issue of whether or not Mosaic Law continued to apply to Christians remained contentious for many centuries (since the 11th century) and remains a great cause of some consternation today among Orthodox leaders.

The Orthodox Church asserts its beginnings in the first century of the Christian era with the birth of Jesus Christ from the Virgin Mary in Bethlehem and notes the fact that he was a rabbi. However, whether converts from among the Gentiles or Jews had to maintain or conform to Mosaic Law (especially the Ten Commandments and circumcision) was at the center of debates in the early church. According to its teachings, the most important decision the church made during the first century was the answer to this question. Initially it was decided that a convert would not be subjected to Mosaic Law, with the exception of the Ten Commandments. Most interesting for this study is the fact that the writings that exist from the third century are the *Teachings of the Apostles* (also called the Didache) from Syria, home of the first Arab immigrants to the United States.

Emperor Constantine's mother, Saint Helen, went to Palestine in the fourth century to make pilgrimage to the holy sites of Christ's life. While on this pilgrimage she discovered near the hill of Golgotha outside Jerusalem the "True Cross" on which Christ was crucified. It was here that

Constantine (a non-Christian at the time) built churches, including the Church of the Holy Sepulcher, thereby making Jerusalem a center of pilgrimage for the Christian world. Constantine became revered for ending Christian persecution among many other contributions to Christian life. He made Sunday a day of worship in addition to Saturday (the Sabbath), creating the weekend that we still have in the West. He exempted clergy from civic duty and formulated a form of welfare for the poor. As emperor of the eastern and western Christian empires, he generally brought peace. Although Constantine managed to quell threats from outside of his empire and arbitrate some of those inside the Christian empire, he was unable to crush all of the schisms.

The Council of Nicea in 325, the first ecumenical council, settled discrepancies over the createdness or uncreatedness of the Logos, the Word and Son of God, by declaring him ever existant and fully divine. Jesus is begotten (born) from the Father and not created by him. Jesus is of one essence with the Father. The council also decreed a number of canons (church regulations) regarding order and discipline. It allowed the churches in major cities to keep jurisdictional authority of their regions and affirmed the propriety of allowing married men to be ordained as deacons and presbyters (elders) and for bishops to have a normal married life. (Celibacy for priests did not become the decree of the Roman Church until the 12th century, though there was previously a tradition of celibacy for monks among Eastern churches.)

The greatest of all the schisms that the church had survived occurred in 1056: the break of communion between the Eastern Orthodox and Catholic Churches. Although there were ecclesiastical (relating to the Christian Church or its clergy) differences and sometimes theological disputes, nothing was as serious as what happened in 1056. Previously there had been language disputes over whether Latin or Greek was the authoritative language for guidance from writings of the church fathers and in liturgy. Of note, the priests, bishops, and scholars of the Eastern churches spoke and wrote in Greek, while the Western church clergy and scholars wrote and spoke in Latin. This is important for access to authoritative writings as a means for guidance for congregations and also attests to struggles for power using language as the tool. Possession of the oldest and most authoritative texts and which language they are in become critical questions.

Orthodox historians list a litany of egregious acts on the part of the Western church, especially around the issue of the church owning land and increasing its wealth; Eastern churches felt that the church should not own land, as this led to greed. Doctrinal issues spotlighted the question of the origin of the Holy Spirit: the Father or the Father and Son? The

Eastern Church did not accept the Western wording that the Holy Spirit "proceeds from" the Father and the Son (Jesus) and instead chose the concept that while the Holy Spirit is also lord, God the Father is the source of all three. This harkens back to initial questions over the role of the Holy Spirit and createdness. In formulating the cosmological under-pinnings of the church, how God makes himself known to creation is of utmost importance. The presence of the Holy Spirit was evident, but its origin was a subject of debate; whether it came directly and only from God or from Jesus or both caused many subsequent debates.

Another debate was over the dating of Easter, which remains a point of division today. During the first few centuries of the church, Eastern Christians had celebrated Easter on the Jewish holiday of Passover. On this subject there was a convergence of opinions of the two branches, as seen in the debates over whether Mosaic Law (as Jesus followed it) was to be a part of Christianity. The Western churches always celebrated Easter on a Sunday. The Eastern practice was condemned in the fourth century, leading to the celebration of Easter at different times all over Christen-dom. By the sixth century, Western Christians' Easter was celebrated on the first Sunday after the first full moon occurring on or after March 21. In the East, Easter is celebrated on the first Sunday following the full moon after vernal equinox but also the Sunday following Passover.

Despite doctrinal and other differences, the break between East and West was sealed with the expulsion of Pope Leo by the patriarch (head of the Eastern Church); the pope then excommunicated the patriarch. This break is still in force today, though Pope Francis, the current pope, has made some overtures to at least a level of cordiality. The nominal head of an Eastern Orthodox Church is the patriarch of Constantinople, who is one among equals; other patriarchs (there are today four patriarchs of the Eastern churches) guide regional churches.

Orthodox Beliefs and Practices

Orthodox (also called Eastern) Christians believe that Lord Jesus Christ handed down divine revelation in oral form, which was later recorded and constituted the founding of their church. The faithful gather under the church's shelter to achieve repentance and forgiveness and to restate their intention to do the will of God. The church is believed to be a place for teaching and sanctification. The congregation constitutes the "royal priesthood."

The Eastern Orthodox Church is considered infallible but is simulta-neously limited in that there is no claim to a total comprehension of all of the intricacies of "the Truth." It must continue to settle controversies and scrutinize what "the Truth" means. Church fathers meet in synods (assemblies of clergy) to discuss disputed issues and to interpret and decree the correct meaning of the "Truth" in question. That "Truth" may include anything from some new knowledge about the origin of the Holy Spirit to new technologies in health care that may cause concern for the church.

Essentials of belief are generally divided into four main parts:

1. Principles of belief and faith;
2. The worship of God, in whom lies belief and hope for salvation;
3. The living of life so as to serve one's neighbor and especially the "least of them" as well as oneself; and
4. The enforcing of a system of order of discipline and administration for the members of this church.

The sacred sources are the Scriptures and sacred apostolic tradition. Jesus Christ is the only redeemer by whom and in whom man's personal salvation is achieved.

The most basic truth of the Orthodox Church is the faith revealed in the true God: the Holy Trinity of the Father, the Son, and the Holy Ghost. The Orthodox community believes that God is both one in substance and triune in three persons or hypostases. Essential to Christ's life (and thus that of Christianity and the beliefs of the church) is his crucifixion, which is then considered the end of his humiliation and emptiness on Earth. The sins of mankind are nailed to the cross; this act is memorialized in the divine event, the sorrows of Easter, which is linked with Jesus's resurrection—the glorification of Christ.

Humankind is conceived of as Godlike, and its corruption was not complete. Man's desire for salvation implies that humankind feels an inner emptiness and is compelled to turn toward God for forgiveness and compassion so as to be regenerated. This regeneration is already a part of God's plan and the reason why Jesus Christ the savior was sent.

Members of the church are sanctified through baptism and chrismation (similar to confirmation in the Catholic Church) along with the ceremony of the Holy Eucharist and confession. The events on this list are called the sacraments. Additionally, there are three other sacraments: ordination, marriage, and unction, which are not obligatory. Only one baptism is allowed, which means that Christians who were baptized in other churches are accepted by dispensation. It is through baptism that all sins are cleansed; the chrismation (also called confirmation) is the confirmation of an adherent's faith and is the "seal of the gift of the Holy Ghost," as stated at the end of the ceremony.

Marriage and Divorce

Marriage is considered both a sacrament and a mystery. There is the betrothal, which includes the exchange of rings, the procession, the declaration of intention, and the lighting of candles. There are readings from the epistle and the gospel, the Blessing of the Common Cup, and the Dance of Isaiah (the bride and groom are led around a table three times). There is no exchange of vows. Spouses are proclaimed the king and queen of a new family. The church understands marriage as a lifelong commitment but also recognizes that there are circumstances when it is unsustainable. Divorce is permitted though not encouraged.

Birth and Death

As in most religious traditions, pregnancy is encouraged in the Eastern Orthodox Church. Birth control is generally accepted except that which would potentially abort a fetus. Reproductive assistance is also accepted but within limits determined by individual churches. The practice of announcing the name of the child was based on the Jewish rite and has recently been reinstated in the prayer service; the names of saints are preferred, as this connects a child to a saint who will pray for him or her throughout life, whether this naming occurs in a naming ceremony or not. On the 40th day after birth, the mother and child are invited to the church for a prayer service to reunite the mother and unite the child to the faith community. This is called the 40-Day Churching, which lasts about 10 minutes and may include chrismation, according to some sources. In contrast, Roman Catholic Church baptism is generally for infants, followed by a first communion usually at puberty and then confirmation during adolescence.

Adoption is acceptable and encouraged. Fornication (including sexual foreplay) is condemned, and both mother and father must take responsibility for the nurturing and sustenance of the child.

All Orthodox Christians are buried, as cremation is forbidden. The body is placed in a casket and set in a grave with a marker or monument with the image of the cross. Organ donation is encouraged, especially as healthy organs are no longer needed for the living.

If possible, a priest is called to the bedside of the gravely ill with the family to sing prayers for God's mercy and for peace for the departing soul. The body is placed in an open casket with a cross placed near the head. The deceased is remembered annually on the anniversary of death.

Orthodox Christian Holidays

The Julian calendar (named after Julius Caesar) took effect in 45 BCE. It was the calendar of most European countries and European settlements in the Americas and elsewhere until 1582, when Pope Gregory replaced it with the Gregorian calendar. Today Western churches follow the Gregorian calendar, while Orthodox (Eastern) churches follow the Julian calendar. There is a difference of 13 days between calendars. For example, for the Western churches, Christmas is December 25; on the Julian calendar, Christmas is January 7. Easter and its related holidays are movable feasts; they do not fall on a fixed date in the Gregorian and Julian calendars.

One major holiday is the celebration of the Virgin Mary's birthday every September, the only woman in Christian history to be given the honor of a holy birth. Preceding the celebration of her birth is a remembrance of her assumption, called the Dormitan Fast.

Easter, the remembrance of the death of Jesus Christ, is preceded by 40 days of self-examination. This is considered the most significant of the holidays. For Orthodox Christians, it begins with a baked specialty, and then there is no meat and dairy until Easter (Pascha). It begins on Clean Monday (a cleansing from sinful attitudes prior to Lent) and ends on Lazarus Saturday (celebrating Jesus's miracle of bringing a man back to life). One week before Easter is Palm Sunday, which commemorates the triumphal entry of Jesus into Jerusalem.

Icons

An icon is a religious work of art that depicts Christ, Mary, saints, and/ or angels. It may be located on the side or back of the pews, on the pulpit, on a windowpane, or elsewhere. Icons are especially prominent in Eastern and Oriental Orthodox church windows and in interior design. They are often also illuminated with a candle in a special jar in churches and homes.

The story of iconography in Christianity is as old as Christianity. While traveling to Jerusalem for his trial and subsequent crucifixion, he received an invitation from a king to him. Since Jesus could not accept the invitation, he sent a linen cloth on which he had dried his face. This began the iconographic tradition. Through the centuries many artists have become famous for their distinctive styles, and their renderings have cultural influences. The images created have sacred value, as they are images of another reality.

Islam: A Brief History

The story of Muslim beliefs and practices lies first and foremost in the Sunni community and then the differences that lie in the branch of Shia Islam. The third branch of Islam (Sufi Islam) will not be discussed here because there are no references to their presence in this group of immigrants. The relationship between Shia and Sunni Islam is one where there are far more similarities than differences, though those differences have made for two different branches of Islam. Sufi Islam will not be discussed here primarily because it was not the faith perspective of the Arab Muslims who migrated to the United States; no mention of it appears in either newspaper or historical accounts.

Islam is the religious tradition of about 1.75 billion people in the world; like Christianity, it can be found on all the inhabitable continents and in almost every country. The people who practice the religion of Islam are called Muslims. "Islam" is an Arabic word meaning "submission" and refers to the surrender of the individual's will to the will of God.

The prophet of Islam, Muhammad ibn Abdullah, was born in Mecca, Arabia, around 570 CE and died in Medina, Arabia, in 632. In Muhammad's time, Arabian society consisted of large tribes bonded by shared ancestry. An elder and a council resolved disputes through negotiations, and consensus ruled within each tribal family and in negotiations with others. Almost all tribes were patriarchal and patrilineal, meaning that not only did political and economic power reside primarily with men but also that children were regarded as the descendants of their father but not of their mother. However, some sources suggest that in some tribes lineage was passed through the mother. Despite the patriarchy, it is also known that some women were wealthy through their own property holdings, perhaps by inheritance.

Arabia had no central government and existed as a collection of tribes and surrounding mercantile and agrarian cities connected by trade. All were heavily dependent on east-west trade routes (between the Indian Ocean and the Mediterranean Sea) and north-south routes (between Africa and the Byzantine Empire).

Historical sources on religious traditions of the tribes in Arabia prior to the prophet of Islam are scarce. The surrounding empires had large Christian communities, while Sassanid Persia was officially Zoroastrian (founded about 3,500 years ago by the prophet Zoroaster; its followers believed in one god called Ahura Mazda). All empires had substantial

Muslim Americans pray during Ramadan at the Islamic Cultural Center in Manhattan, New York, in 2011. (Robert Nickelsberg/Getty Images)

Jewish populations. Arabs had no formal religion but believed in a combination of supernatural forces called either spirits or gods. In the absence of religious codes, the population was governed by a series of social rules and values such as honor, courage, and hospitality. The people revered poetry and esteemed "good" poets who told the ancestral history, along with soothsayers (fortune-tellers) and judges.

Into this environment, a prophet was born who was orphaned early in life and raised by a foster family, a grandfather, and then an uncle. Each of these guardians is said to have contributed to his stable, inwardly thoughtful, and honest personality. While he was working as a trader, these qualities led Khadijah, a wealthy widower and an owner of caravans, to ask for his hand in marriage. Though his wife was at least 15 years his senior, their marriage by all accounts was quiet and productive; their family consisted of several children. The boys died in infancy; several girls survived. During one of his retreats to a mountain cave outside Mecca, Muhammad received his first revelation at 40 years of age. This is the revelation that all of Arabia had of the existence of God, more powerful than all of their spirits and gods combined.

This potential societal and thus economic and political disruption to the standing ordering of society and its many tribes caused immediate persecution of Muhammad, his family, and the few followers who had come to believe in the revelations. The first revelations put authority with God rather than tribal elders and turned attention away from the fatalism that had previously described human existence—we live and then we die, and what lives on are the stories of our deeds. The depth of the persecution, which included a largely successful withholding of the ability to procure food, led to what is called the first immigration of a small number of Muslims to Abyssinia, where they were welcomed and housed by its king. Those remaining behind continued to survive under cruel oppression that led to a large emigration from Mecca to Yathrib (modern-day Medina), about 280 miles away. In 622 the prophet Muhammad had been offered the opportunity to become a judge there, and he agreed to do so if his family and followers moved with him, would be supported until they could provide for themselves, and would be considered full citizens of the city with protection in case the armies of Mecca followed them. The year 622, called the Hijra, is an especially important date in Islamic history, and it marks the beginning of the Islamic calendar and the beginning of Islam as a social religion and political entity.

Those Meccan armies did follow, and Islamic history is full of stories of the resultant conflicts, with the Muslims winning some wars and not others. Nevertheless, the revelations continued, and the community of Muslims continued to grow. Finally, in 630 after almost eight years of fighting, Mecca surrendered. Little retribution was claimed except for the most persistent of those who ridiculed and carried out campaigns against the prophet and his followers. The Kaaba, the central house of the many spirits and deities worshipped by various tribes, was cleansed and emptied. It became the central focus of Islamic pilgrimage.

Throughout history, Prophet Muhammad's subsequent marriages after the death of his first wife of 25 years have been highly scrutinized. Muslim scholars agree that almost all of these marriages were political in that they cemented bonds between tribes and the message of Islam. This common way of securing loyalty, allies, and hospitality was not protested during its time, and marriage as a way of securing wealth is still common today.

After the death of Prophet Muhammad, issues arose over who would succeed him—one of the prophet's tribe who was a relative or someone of another clan who had also been with the prophet and proven their loyalty. The former won out; the first caliphs were all of the prophet's tribe and had been with him in the early days of revelation. According to bloodlines (sanguinity), however, the first successor would have been Ali, the cousin and son-in-law of the prophet. Some members of the early community held this belief firm above all else. Overruled, the older early followers of Islam were chosen to lead the community as political representatives.

The belief that Ali should have been the caliph after the death of Prophet Muhammad was held by a minority faction in the community and came into fruition with his selection as the fourth caliph. Ali was seen by this minority as having both a spiritual life and an intimacy, since he had been in Prophet Muhammad's household when the prophet was receiving revelation. This minority of followers saw in Ali a spiritual guidance, not prophecy based on sanguinity, that would lead the community of believers both spiritually and politically.

The majority of the community saw itself as better served by the cousin, Muawiyah, of the third caliph, Uthman. A civil war ensued in which the followers of Muawiyah murdered Ali. This led to the first Islamic dynasty of the descendants of Uthman, the Umayyad dynasty. However, the followers of Ali grew and set up a community elsewhere. A later conflict at Karbala, led by Muawiyah's son, led to the massacre of Ali's son Husayn and his family and servants. One of the special memorials of Shia Islam is a commemoration of the massacre at Karbala. Both branches of Islam, Sunni and Shia, believe that the murder of the fourth Imam closed the period of a particular kind of legitimate caliphate, although they disagree on the nature of the legitimacy.

The word Qur'ān is derived from the Arabic verb meaning "to read" or "to recite"—a collection of things to be recited or a recitation. For the majority of believers, the Arabic Qur'ān is Allah's word transmitted to humanity through Prophet Muhammad by way of the angel Jibrīl (Gabriel). The prophet would receive a portion of revelation and recite it to those around him. The text is arranged in 114 suras (fixed enclosures) of unequal length subdivided into *ayat* (signs; sing. *ayah*). The Qur'ān was spoken by Prophet Muhammad after each revelation and memorized by those in the community. In communities known for their prodigious memories, this was no feat of consequence and not difficult at all. The revelations were also written from memory on whatever available materials were at hand. The pieces were methodically collected after the death of the prophet and compiled into one text—not, however, in the chronological order of revelation. Perhaps during Prophet Muhammad's lifetime there were other attempts to compile the revelations, but there is no evidence of this assertion.

Muslims all over the world memorize portions of the Qur'ān, especially for recitation during prayers and on special occasions. A significant number of men and women memorize the entirety of the text, reciting large portions daily to keep the memory fresh. The Qur'ān has been translated into at least 114 languages. Similar to Catholic Christianity and Judaism,

Islam has law. Unlike Christianity but like Judaism, there are supplementary texts that believers study. The life of Prophet Muhammad is so central that those written narratives of what he said and did on specific occasions are held in high esteem and provide some context for the law.

The word "hadith" refers to a communication or a narrative. For Muslims, it means a narrative record of the sayings of Prophet Muhammad and his companions, while the sunna is a record of his manner of living. It is in this way that a new tradition was instituted, since the old tradition of following in the ways of one's ancestors had to be abandoned as followers had to turn away from belief in the gods of the Kaaba and in the deeds of their ancestors for guidance. Codifying this new tradition led to a new era of literary sciences; the sciences of other subjects also emerged, and the literate began to set down the rules for engagement among themselves and newly Arabized tribes. Of course, as new communities of peoples came into the Muslim sphere, they not only brought their own cultural interpretations but also made additions to the corpus of hadith literature that served their communities. Thus, according to many scholars, the majority of hadith accounts cannot be regarded as reliable historical accounts of the sunna of the prophet. This situation ushered in a science of hadith authentication whereby for a hadith to be considered authentic, the chain of transmission had to be checked, verified, and validated according to a schema.

The sunna is asserted to contain the manner of living of the prophet of Islam—his actions and sayings in response to questions or events. Since hadith literature contains the sunna, it is only natural that hadith literature in Shia Islam is different in the transmitters of the traditions, not in the methodology for identifying them, and thus somewhat different in focus regarding worship and the place of women, for example.

Islamic law (sharia) is a system of laws used as guiding principles to reason through the resolution of conflict, wrongs, and the punishment of crimes in the lives of many Muslims. The foundational principles for the theory of law are found in the Qur'ān and include guidance on worship, dietary rules, and the distribution of inheritance property. However, as new cultures and situations arose, the necessity of creating a system to handle the issues became paramount. This system of principles of jurisprudence is called *fiqh,* which includes actual case law.

Beliefs and Practices

Islam has a particularly developed set of beliefs and rituals, which are required by all practicing Muslims. Scholars during the eighth and ninth centuries wrote down what was required to be considered Muslim, probably in direct response to the rapid spread of Islam in the world. The central requirements revolved around belief in the unity of God, revelation, and prophecy.

All practicing Muslims are required to believe in the oneness of God (Allah) and that Allah is unique and eternal. Allah created the universes and all that is in them. Humans were created with the capacity to do good as well as evil, with the ability to choose between them. Allah is unlike anything in the created world, and it is an unforgivable disobedience to ascribe partners to Allah. Allah has no gender and is omnipresent and omniscient.

Prophets are of two types: those who have a mission from Allah to warn their communities and simultaneously to inform them of Allah's Will and those who have the added responsibility of bringing a revelation. Muslims believe in a series of prophets that include prophets claimed in the scriptures of Judaism and Christianity. Muhammad is considered the last prophet to humankind; Jesus is seen as the Messiah and born of the Virgin Mary. However, Muslims do not believe that Allah is the father of Jesus.

It is believed that Allah used prophets to reveal himself to humankind, and thus Muslims believe in four scriptures—the Torah, the Psalms, the Injil (portions of the New Testament), and the Qur'ān. It is understood that the substance of these texts in their original form is the same; differences between them are ascribed to tampering, loss, or the era of translation compromising the intent of the text.

There is also a belief that angels exist and are used by Allah to perform tasks such as bringing scriptures to prophets. Angels are beings that cannot disobey Allah, and at least two of them are charged with recording an individual's deeds, good and bad.

The afterlife or Day of Judgment is another central Islamic belief. This life is lived as a test of an individual's commitment to living a good life. At the end of earthly time judgment of all human beings will occur, and rewards and punishments will be meted out.

All Muslims believe that Islam was sent as the final religion for humankind. The first step in belief is the profession of the Shahadah, which is a witnessing that there is no god but Allah and that Muhammad is the last prophet of Allah. This profession of faith is to be a voluntary and conscious declaration of an individual's beliefs. It is understood that other monotheists could utter the first part of this declaration, but the second part is what distinguishes the Muslim. The Shahadah is recited at least nine times daily as a part of the five daily prayers.

Salat (prayers) are performed just before daybreak, just after the sun has reached the highest point in the sky, in the middle of the afternoon, just after sunset, and after it is dark, comprising 17 units of movement. It is important to note that Shia Muslims perform all the prayers but distribute the 17 units differently, combining the two midday prayers and the evening and night prayers. Fasting is practiced by both Shia and Sunni Muslims, with nothing taken by mouth from sunrise to sunset for 29 or 30 days during the lunar month of Ramadan by those who have reached puberty and are able. This fast is one of self-restraint not only from eating or drinking but also from unnecessary worldly pleasures and intimate relations with spouses.

Zakat is an annual tax at around 2.5 percent on earnings on beyond-living expenses from the previous year, paid at the end of Ramadan. It is a reminder that all wealth comes from Allah and that to share with the needy and less fortunate is incumbent on believers in the Muslim community as their situations permit.

The pilgrimage to Mecca (hajj) is a journey required at least once in a lifetime to the birthplace of historical Islam for those physically able and who are financially capable (meaning they can support their families during their absence). This pilgrimage lasts a week, from the 9th through the 13th of the 12th month of the Muslim lunar calendar (10 weeks after the end of Ramadan). Sufi, Shia, and Sunni Muslims from around the world make this journey annually, enabling an exchange of ideas and knowledge from all parts of the world. Remarkably, the over 2 million people annually who make this trip in contemporary times are relatively orderly in what could otherwise be a Tower of Babel, mediated by the common language of the Arabic Qur'ān.

Marriage, Polygyny, Temporary Marriage, and Divorce

Marriage in Islam is a legal contractual agreement. The Qur'ān contains directives regarding who may marry, along with guidance on the rights and duties of spouses. Contracts are negotiated prior to marriage with attention to duties and rights, along with conditions for divorce and the amount and kind of dowry to be paid to the wife. This dowry payment is due at the time of the marriage; without it, there is no contract and thus no marriage. In many Muslim cultures, this essential part of marriage has been postponed or otherwise neglected, causing innumerable problems for couples. Actual marriage ceremonies are cultural, with the legal contractual portion taking place separately from the ceremonial aspects.

Prevailing and majority interpretations of the Qur'ān assert that Islamic law permits a man to marry up to four women at one time, as such social conditions may dictate. While there is the encouragement to treat them equally, there is an equal assertion by the Qur'ān that this is not possible and that monogamy is the best. Despite this advice, polygyny is practiced in almost all Muslim-majority states and some Muslim-minority states, though it is not legally permitted in most.

Temporary marriage (*mut'ah*) is a practice of Shiism. It is important to note that in contemporary times, temporary marriage is considered taboo in most communities. Nevertheless, Shiism bases its permission on instances of temporary marriages that happened in the early years of Islam. Shia Muslims assert that this practice continued until its banning a few years after the death of Muhammad. Temporary marriages also have contracts that stipulate duties and rights of the marriage and especially the length of the contract. Clearly, the issues for women posed by temporary marriage greatly influenced its relegation to the category of taboo.

Islamic law allows for the possibility of divorce, and there is the expectation, although it is not generally the case, that its conditions have been negotiated in the marriage contract. It is far easier for men to divorce women than for women to divorce men. Women can, however, sue for divorce. Divorce is frowned upon, and families usually make extensive efforts to prevent it.

Death and Funerals

Muslims view death as the culmination of the phase of earthly life, at which time they enter a liminal state until the Day of Judgment. Here they answer for their actions in this world. Those with good deeds and actions go to Paradise, while those who have not believed or whose actions are morally wrong go to the hellfire.

Family members will attempt to make sure that the dying are facing the direction of the Kaaba in Mecca, and if able, they recite the Shahadah and some part of the Qur'ān. Muslims are supposed to be buried within a day of their death in most Muslim-majority countries, but the circumstances of death or the distance of relatives may extend this time.

The body is ritually bathed after death by family or, in the absence of family, by those assigned this task by the community. Bodies are not embalmed or dressed but are perfumed, wrapped in a shroud, and, in the United States, placed in caskets, which are never opened. Funeral services are generally simple, consisting of carrying the body to the mosque, making ritual prayers, and then proceeding to the grave site for burial.

Islamic Holidays

Holidays follow the lunar calendar and so occur at different times each year. Eid al-Fitr (Feast of Breaking the Fast) is celebrated on the first day of the new month about 10 weeks after the month of Ramadan. The entire community gathers for a special prayer that morning and generally celebrates for the next three days. The second *eid* is actually the more important of the two. Eid al-Adha (Feast of the Sacrifice) is the holiest of the holidays and marks the culmination of the hajj. This holiday falls on the 10th day of the final month of the Islamic calendar. The major feature of this holiday is the sacrifice of animals, which commemorates Prophet Abraham's willingness to sacrifice his son, Ishmael, in obedience to Allah's command. The meat is consumed and/or given to charity.

The first month of the Islamic calendar is Muharram; it has become synonymous with a mourning ritual practiced by the largest group of Shia Muslims. Muharram commemorates the martyrdom of Prophet Muhammad's cousin Ali and his son (and Muhammad's grandson) Husayn. This event lasts 10 days.

The Alawis

The Alawis are a branch of the majority branch of Shia Islam, the Twelvers, who have been centered in Syria since the ninth century. Alawism combines elements of other traditions into its theology and philosophy and is generally thought to be deviant by the mainstream of Shia Islam. Alawis too were oppressed as a community during the Ottoman Empire through attempts to convert them to Sunni Islam. Their response was to periodically rise up against the empire from their mountain habitat, where they could maintain some autonomy.

To have some control over the community, Ottomans employed some of them as tax collectors, conscripts in the Ottoman wars with Egypt, and governors over specific regions. Alawis have been subject to the various occupations of Syria, and they adapted. Syria became independent in 1946, and after a series of coups the Alawis came to power in 1966 and continue to hold it through the turmoil of today. Despite the hold on power, Alawis also immigrated to the United States.

Religions from the East and the Pluralism of America

By the time Arab Christians and Muslims came to the United States, politicians had defined the nature of religious protections in the First

Amendment of the U.S. Constitution and the permissible role of religion in American public life. Though many Americans rely on those First Amendment protections, few can accurately recite the amendment or what it prohibits. The First Amendment is "equally dedicated to preventing the establishment of religion and to protecting the rights of freedom of religious conscience and practice for all citizens" (notes taken from a lecture by Judge Anthony Simpkins, December 2016). This amendment is at the core of civic life in America. There is no established religion, though the founding faith, Protestant Christianity, had made its mark on holidays, money, and public discourse. The protection of the rights of religious conscience and practice for all permits people of other faiths to come to America and practice their faith without governmental interference unless that practice somehow endangers the public space.

Despite the separation of church and state, religious activity in the public spaces is intense and competitive. The presence of diverse traditions makes for an interesting marketplace. Until its exposure to evangelical Protestantism, Islam was only known for introducing itself to those who wanted to know. Orthodox Christianity met evangelical Protestantism and closed its doors. Muslims coming to America had never been involved in proselytization and did not engage in it until the last decade or two of the 20th century. Nevertheless, both communities were seen as potential competitors in the marketplace of salvation. Hinduism and Buddhism joined the religious market in the later 20th century.

Profile

Salim Caraboolad (?–?) came to Cleveland in 1892 from Lebanon. He organized and was president of the St. George Society, a fraternal organization. This organization was an aid society to assist new immigrants in settling, getting legal aid, applying for citizenship, registering to vote, and voting. Caraboolad was instrumental in the establishment of St. Elias Church, which ministered to Melkite Catholics, Maronite Catholics, and Orthodox in the Ohio area.

References

Erickson, John H. *Orthodox Christians in America: A Short History.* Religion in American Life. Oxford: Oxford University Press, 2007.

McGuckin, John Anthony. *The Orthodox Church: An Introduction to Its History, Doctrine, and Spiritual Culture.* New York: Wiley-Blackwell, 2010.

Suleiman, Michael W., ed. *Arabs in America: Building a New Future.* Philadelphia: Temple University Press, 1999.

CHAPTER FIVE

Political Organizing and Engagement

Arab Americans began political organizing in 1912 when workers were in the forefront of a strike of some 25,000 textile workers in Lawrence, Massachusetts. Arab Americans have been an integral and significant component of the Detroit automotive industry since its inception. They have been leaders and officers in the International Union, United Automobile, Aerospace and Agricultural Implement Workers of America (UAW) and in the 1970s organized the Arab Workers' caucus within the UAW initially for the purpose of protesting the union's buying of Israeli bonds and later for Democratic Party activism.

A number of organizations emerged from the express need to have at least some voice in explaining various Arab-Israeli wars and conflicts, especially after the Six-Day War (1967). The Association of Arab-American University Graduates was formally launched in 1967, the National Association of Arab Americans emerged to devote itself to lobbying in 1972, and the strictly political Arab-American Anti-Discrimination Committee gave strident voice against patterns of prejudice and discrimination in 1980. The Arab American Institute, which functions in many ways across the cultural and political spectrum, was formed in 1985.

Despite the broad organizational foundation that these organizations provided, they did not translate into political incorporation. Writers have referred to Arab Americans, along with Catholics and Japanese, as historically having held only alien citizenship, which is formal citizenship coupled with a feeling of being viewed as aliens by mainstream American society. Some of these feelings are still held, though Catholics have

Lawrence, Massachusetts, mill workers' strike in 1912. (Library of Congress)

certainly become the exception, holding six U.S. Supreme Court seats. Arab Americans have not reached these pinnacles yet, which may be due to their small population numbers.

The post–9/11 environment in the United States made life even more difficult. The Federal Bureau of Investigation (FBI) reported a 1,600 percent increase in anti-Arab crimes from 2000 to 2001. Particular immigrants, mostly from Arab or Muslim countries, were required to register with the federal government. Add to this the racial profiling that came with the USA Patriot Act, and there was little chance of increasing the political presence of Arabs during this time. Yet there is a positive side to all of this.

The increased Arab baiting led to increased access to governmental agencies and their services. Some agencies found that they had to attempt to undo the harm they had caused. This harm also caused other historically racially challenged groups, such as the Japanese, to come to their aid. They knew the potential harm of detention camps and provided counseling and even joined protest marches in some communities such as Chicago.

Political participation has remained a mostly male prerogative, as many women have no hereditary memory of women in office. Younger women, however, are interested in politics and are beginning to use what they learn from working in community organizations as a springboard into political participation. Although political participation is slowly increasing, preoccupation with Arab-Israeli affairs continues to be a priority. What has not been a priority is lobbying Arab nations to resolve conflicts.

There has been no lobbying to speak against terrorism beyond statements joining others in condemning terrorism. Some leaders have cautioned against speaking out against terrorism, as this might dilute their efforts in matters revolving around Palestine. This dilemma is increasingly being challenged as young adults see their stake in America as a priority. The current efforts by U.S. president Donald Trump to ban Muslim immigration and put those with visas or green cards under extreme vetting may propel Arab Americans into political participation.

The very particular ban on refugees, immigrants, green card holders, and those with visas from seven predominantly Arab Muslim countries turned a campaign promise to ban Muslims from entering the country into a reality. The number of Americans, including lawyers, who saw this as a violation of the U.S. Constitution was significant. The shortsightedness of this ban was quickly revealed as physicians, students, lawful residents, and others were caught up in the mix. The public outcry was enormous, although there were many supporters of the president who felt that all Muslims should be banned from entry regardless of the consequences.

Trump wanted to admit Christians from these same countries because they had been persecuted. Judges and lawyers challenged the ban and won a retraction, returning some normalcy but only for a short time. The Trump administration immediately crafted another ban, which left out some of the specific religious references but was essentially the same; judges in at least two jurisdictions again blocked it. What has since been put in place is extreme vetting of people coming from predominantly Arab states into the United States. The enormous consequences and inconveniences for business and student travelers have yet to be assessed.

Social Organization

Paradoxically, the few large Arab American organizations find themselves in competition with smaller groups that have arisen after 9/11 and more recently during the previous presidential campaign season with its anti-Arab/anti-Muslim rhetoric. About one-third of Arab Americans, 300,000 out of 1.5 million, are Palestinian and see that much of the political and social activism around American issues can take away from or diminish the focus on Arab-Israeli issues. This tension prevents some obvious alliances among groups. The end result is a diminution of presence in the public square. Younger Arab Americans are signaling the diversity of the community and thus a variety of concerns and more willingness to compromise and form alliances.

Arab Americans continue to feel that one most important aspect of living in America is the protection of Arab values. Second to this concern has always been an attempt to influence U.S. policy on the Middle East, which changed significantly after the death of Yasser Arafat in 2004 and the ensuing series of Palestinian attacks on Israel. The Arab Spring in 2010 shifted the focus of Arabs from the Israeli conflict to the oppressions of Arab leadership in each individual state. After 9/11 and now with direct assaults on the integrity of the Arab American community, this divided focus on the continuing unrest remains. Arab refugees from aggregate unrest and economic collapse are flooding Europe and Turkey, causing rising anti-Arab sentiments across the world.

One of the world's worst terrorist groups is predominantly Arab, and its assaults on other Arabs casts aspersions on Arab Americans. Again, Arab Americans find themselves entangled with overseas chaos, anti-Arab rhetoric, and one aspect of the center of hate. Nonetheless, some members of the community have distinguished themselves.

Leading medical teams of physicians and nurses, including Syrian American doctors such as Mohammed Sahloul, made underground hospitals in Syria and saved lives. In the process they have alerted the general American community to the differences among Arabs and to their prominence in the health care arena. Alongside this initiative, Arab lawyers have joined the American Civil Liberties Union (ACLU) to assist, free of charge, those caught in Trump's ban. Proving who you are is interestingly as difficult as proving who you are not in this case. Every time an Arab anywhere commits an act of terrorism, all Arabs are summarily accused.

Members of the Arab community are learning that the best way to protect their values is to share with and learn from others. One fear of every immigrant community is integration. For those who have come from countries of chaos and war, the fear of losing identity is perhaps even greater.

Cultural Organization

The diversity of Arab Americans is seen more and more in various interactions with other Americans. Arab Americans are bringing their countries' music, literature, and even sports to the United States. Productive collaborations are seen most often in music and poetry. Cultural centers and galleries now number at least 27 around the country. These entities cosponsor film festivals, host concerts, and support new artists. All of these efforts draw on the rich traditions of the Middle East in every field of the arts. Centers also teach Arabic to children and adults.

The Inner-City Muslim Action Network

The Inner-City Muslim Action Network (IMAN) is a community organization that fosters health, wellness, and healing in the inner city by organizing for social change. IMAN operates a holistic health center; provides transitional housing and job training for formerly incarcerated men; hosts a community café that connects local, national, and international arts in storytelling, music, dance, and visual arts; and runs a corner store campaign to clean up a particularly underserviced area of Chicago. The café provides a platform for not only artistic expression but also cross-cultural dialogue, civic engagement, and social change.

IMAN's founder, Dr. Rami Nashashibi, works tirelessly to make a place available for young adults (Muslim or not) to engage in productive endeavors and to determine their self-representation in civic life in light of negative stereotypes.

Typically, museums will chart the history of Arabs in the local setting and then the region, including where they settled and what their achievements were. Cultural and community centers are places of wedding, graduation, and birthday parties. Some even hold cooking classes open to all. Cultural centers hold town hall meetings on knowing rights as well as how to represent the community to media sources and provide assistance to new immigrants.

The War on Terror

The U.S. government assumes that how it deals with the Middle East can be applied at home with Arab Americans. As the U.S. developed the parameters for fighting the war on terror, it also developed parameters for fighting counterterrorism and the homegrown actors that it assumed to be among youths and young adult Arab American males. They became the objects to be surveilled, as they were viewed as being susceptible to radicalization and violent extremism.

Ironically, these descriptors were used successfully in the past against Native Americans and Japanese Americans and more recently against

Mexican American youths, though the strategies for neutralization were different. Native American children were taken from their parents and put in boarding schools "to instill the values of civilization and to erase any vestiges of their native culture" (Sirin and Fine 2008, 66). Japanese youths were sent with their parents to detention camps to emphasize the exclusion of their culture from the fabric of American life. The psychological damages are still being felt in subsequent generations today. The question of roots is a real one. The term "Native Americans" is a misnomer; the preferred term among Native Americas is "First Nation," since despite exclusion they are indeed the true owners of this land. Japanese Americans have passed down the trauma of their internment through the generations, and their vows to never let that dehumanization happen to anyone else has drawn them close to Arab American parents.

The war on terror has produced many conflicting strategies. On the one hand, youths are to be protected and encouraged to be innovative; on the other hand, they are to be monitored, contained, repressed, and if necessary deported or detained indefinitely. Though these strategies have been used for many decades against college students involved in causes such as Vietnam War protests and the civil rights movement, the harm caused by the many arms of surveillance on the psyche are immeasurable.

The Stories

Many young Arab Americans dreamed of gaining admission to Ivy League colleges and were careful to keep their grades up, participate in sports, and join student government organizations while in high school. These students' most pressing priorities before 9/11 included passing advanced classes. At home parents, often of mixed cultural backgrounds (such as a Palestinian married to a Moroccan or a Libyan married to an American), schooled them in Arab culture and its values. Most often they were not permitted to date, go to weekend parties, or attend coed school events that lasted beyond 10:00 p.m. in an attempt to keep them bound to Arab values. Some of them even participated in interfaith groups. They already lived a kind of dual existence.

Understanding how your ethnic and religious community is different created angst after 9/11. Young people who were college bound began to deal with the suspicious atmosphere that surrounded them. Their adherence to ethnic and religious demands, such as participating in the Arab American Association or going to the Muslim youth center along with their regular school duties, now provided additional stress.

Researchers have asserted that there is a transition from elementary school to high school regarding friendships. Elementary school friendships are usually well formed and last over a period of years. High schools, however, draw students from a number of different schools; the ordeal of making new friends is thus new, and friends are fewer. Arab girls who decide to cover their hair usually do so during high school. Before 9/11, the scarf was often nothing more than a source of curiosity from friends. After 9/11 suspicion was attached to it, along with exclusions of many types. The Arabic term *hijab* denotes a barrier, and many non-Muslim students see it that way.

Young Arab Muslim women also struggle with the popular notion that the scarf is a symbol of oppression chosen for them. Some say that putting on a scarf was their choice. This "choice" often comes under scrutiny when it is learned that it is a family and community expectation. Others say that their choice is not to wear a scarf because their religiosity does not depend on it.

Given the importance placed on physical appearance in the U.S. racial configuration, Arabs and Pakistanis are readily identified as Muslims and thus have borne the brunt of the suspicions against Muslims after 9/11. Even though the majority of Muslims do not attend mosque, the life of the mosque is attributed to them. The notion of religious freedom that permeates America is not lost on Arab Americans and Muslims. The diversity of interpretations of religious texts and attendant ideologies provide a unique community from which response to terrorism is expected. Each Arab culture adopts a version of Islam that best fits its previous religious practices. This includes those who were secular in the Arab world.

One focus of the American government and thus of many Americans is on those Arabs who practice interpretations of Islamic texts that support war against non-Muslims. Although this is a tiny minority of Arabs, suspicion has been cast on all. Many Arab Americans, like many Jewish Americans, see organized religion as a divisive factor in life and prefer to spend their time on social justice issues.

Political activism, though relatively new, has been a mainstay of youths and young adults since 9/11. This activism has been both identity-based and rights-based. Identity has been formulated around religious and/or ethnic identity, while rights narratives have been focused on civil and human rights. Like many other immigrant groups, Muslims have imported their internal conflicts to the United States. Many families fled the civil unrest and wars among various Muslim groups. Youths and young adults are beginning to decide which issues are their priorities.

Civic participation in the United States is usually learned at a young age from parental civic participation. For immigrants coming from countries where there is no democratic participation in policy or even not-for-profit organizational formation, civics is to be learned. For many youths, parents are scared of the positive and risk-taking behaviors associated with activism. Parental memories of persecution in the ancestral homeland provide anxiety about any activism of their children.

Civic participation is diverse. Those who participate are not following past patterns of name changes or hiding religious adherence to escape mistreatment, nor are they quiet. They are instead proclaiming their ethnic ancestry proudly along with their religious seating. According to a poll in 2004, 82 percent of those responding were registered to vote. Current political trends have encouraged even those who were hesitant but qualified to vote to join registration teams. Intermarriages and social contacts have enlarged their activism beyond problems in the Middle East. Issues in the Middle East now become one of their concerns as opposed to their only concern.

Organizations that previously only served one group of Muslims have expanded their focus to serve Muslims writ large. Some of the organizations, recognizing the push of the young, have made alliances with similar organizations. These efforts have brought young people of different religious backgrounds into the same meetings and events. Yet, the psychological trauma of young people has not been adequately addressed.

One researcher says that the level of psychic disturbance reminded him of that explained in Frantz Fanon's *Black Skin, White Masks*. This text, which describes the "painful shock of seeing oneself through objectifying eyes," talks about negative glances and undue attention (Sirin and Fine 2008, 85). The constant need to cope and protect oneself against hostile forces more real than imagined can wreak chaos on childhoods. These researchers were amazed at the degree to which youths in the study had absorbed various discriminatory acts into their lives. Girls absorbed the stares and sometimes hateful remarks about their scarves, while young adult males absorbed questions when they grew beards.

Many undergraduate Arab and Muslim students in public and private universities experience psychological conditions on campus that experts are now calling "culture-related stress." A variety of discomforting issues arise on college campuses, including sexuality, human rights, and religious beliefs. Discussions lead to competing ways of thinking about issues. Outliers are typically listened to with awe, and sometimes insensitive comments are made. For example, those women who think that sex before

Omar Offendum, Syrian American rapper/poet, performing in 2013. (PYMCA/ Avalon/UIG via Getty Images)

marriage is prohibited (including some Christian women) are many times made fun of by women who are having sex before marriage.

Stress levels are also heightened in professor-student interaction when Arab or Muslim students have to ask for exceptions for papers or need to address some aspersion made about their culture. While college and its rigors intimidate most undergraduates, generally cultural discrimination is not prominent. This kind of discrimination has layers. Young Arabs are surveilled by the FBI for suspicious behavior, and their behavior is under scrutiny by family and community members. They have no place to hide. Years of surveillance have taken their toll.

Many young adults have channeled their frustrations into volunteer work with local organizations, especially charities. Others have put themselves wholeheartedly into becoming hyper-American, while still others have become hyper-Muslim, learning everything they can about Islamic studies through online classes and more formal classes around the nation. Arab American hip-hop has been a major vehicle for expressions of hope and refusal to give in to intimidations.

Artists such as Omar Offendum, Narcyist, and Native Deen have explicitly linked international unrest to American urban unrest, especially in America and the Middle East, and have shown how negotiations through artistry can mediate. A great deal of hip-hop speaks about black poverty in North America, specifically about the hold that street culture has on young people, asking them to challenge the situation. This form is now used to challenge the role that governments play in oppression and also the experiences of immigrant-descended youths in their bicultural world. Non-Muslim American youths listen and in many ways find their voice to still at least some of the frustration of everyday life.

Making a Way through Obstacles

Arab American youths and young adults have begun to avail themselves of the discourses and practical actions of other ethnic minorities. Though the prejudices inside their own communities continue to prove difficult to overcome, their increasing persistence and consistency will win out. They have spent almost all of their lives being stereotyped, undervalued, subject to suspicion, and fearful of the next deportation and feeling generally unsafe. Civics and political education have not been a mainstay of the community, and thus there is little to no legacy to use as a resource. The lives of others become increasingly important.

Sunaina Maira researched and interviewed some in this 9/11 set of generations, with remarkable attention to the nuances of identity building and rights literacy. One focal point is the black struggle for civil rights.

The founding fathers of the United States wrote about humanity's inalienable rights to life, liberty, and the pursuit of happiness, but many did not believe that this should apply to blacks or women; it should only apply to white property-owning males. Needless to say, some white women of means were not pleased with this set of affairs and began suffrage movements in earnest after the emancipation of slaves in the 19th century. Former slaves, on the other hand, had no money to serve as advocates. The old system of abject slavery morphed into sharecropping and only a few years later into a Jim Crow system of segregation and disenfranchisement.

Perpetual poverty accompanied sharecropping on farms in the South, while Jim Crow instituted an almost perpetual system of definite second-class citizenship. The ignominy of being forced into an existence in which the threat of death always hovered lasted almost 100 years after the end of slavery. Lynchings and burnings of black towns such as Rosewood, Florida, and Tulsa, Oklahoma, became permanent stains on American history.

The civil rights movement was actually a collection of movements. Some of these movements emerged from the black church tradition and were subsumed under the leadership of Reverend Martin Luther King Jr.; others were not religiously based and had more socialist overtones. The stories and subsequent discourses that are the legacy of these movements include somewhat sanitized songs of overcoming some day, but the pictures of black children being spat on while integrating schools and police using fire hydrant hoses and dogs to break up marches remain.

What Arab and Muslim young people are gleaning from this rich history is not its horrors, violence, or degradation but instead the fashion of it all at the moment. Protests that meet little violence, no dogs, no spitting, and no jail time are not up to the caliber of a fight for civil rights. However, the increasing study of the movement (and conversations about it) is bound to yield a sense of the philosophy of struggle and the unyielding commitments that must be made. This takes the steadiness of small steps first.

In this stage, young people are absorbing the language of civil rights along with breaking taboos about being in the ghetto. A significant number of Palestinian parents and grandparents found that black and Latino families in urban America in the 1960s and 1970s were welcoming and understanding of their plight in the Middle East. They stayed in those urban spaces until they could make the move to more affluent white areas. The social hierarchy of racially infused America came into full view, and they elected to not get involved in the racial politics of the time. For them, seeing some of their children and grandchildren choose to become directly involved was scary.

The language of civil rights, with its emphasis on the dignity of every human and their God-given right to liberty, is attuned to the plight not only of Palestinians but also of other Arabs seeking relief from chaos. The framework of language provided by the civil rights struggles of various ethnic minorities indeed provides a beginning frame for a struggle against Islamophobia and increasing racism.

Given the foundational racism that undergirds the nation, the struggles of nonwhite citizens are built in, tolerated, resisted, and then encouraged as part of the ongoing experiment of democracy. This cycle is cloaked by the seemingly limitless ability to pursue liberties and is also part of the framework to be resisted. This cycle emerged over time and is so well hidden that most times the struggling minority group does not see it initially. Each injection of struggle has produced either policies or court rulings that resist the bait. For example, the internment of Japanese in the aftermath of the bombing of Pearl Harbor opened a conversation on what the government can and cannot do regarding citizens deemed suspect.

In *Korematsu v. United States* (1944), the U.S. Supreme Court decided that the government order to exclude all Japanese persons from the West Coast aligned with our Constitution, even as it noted that any racial restriction of rights is always "suspect." This case still holds as binding legal precedent today, with dangerous implications for our present and future—particularly as it becomes increasingly cited as a model for policy rather than a disgraceful relic of the past.

As Justice Robert H. Jackson noted in his dissent, "The Court for all time has validated the principle of racial discrimination in criminal procedure and of transplanting American citizens. The principle then lies about like a loaded weapon ready for the hand of any authority that can bring forward a plausible claim of an urgent need" (Ariens 2012, 571).

Dr. Naomi Paik, an assistant professor of Asian studies at the University of Illinois, Urbana-Champaign, in her book *Rightlessness,* reminded readers of the fragility of struggle in the quote above and further asserted how this conversation was extremely important for the Arab and Muslim community. Many influential pundits in the current government feel that Arabs, Muslims, and Islam are the enemy and should be interned or deported, and they definitely should be banned from entering the United States. A language frame already exists (as stated above in Jackson's dissent) to persuade the American public of the urgent need.

While America is perceived as an open country, there is also a perception that too many ethnic voices from the world are poisoning the country with endless demands on its infrastructure. But these are particular ethnic voices. The ethnic voices of Britain, Russia, and the European Union are not perceived as troublesome voices, while those of Spanish and Arabic speakers are. Clearly, in America there is the firm notion of civil liberties. The question is, to whom do they refer? Do civil liberties reference all citizens? Are civil liberties only for some citizens? Does the banner of protection of civil liberties apply to all who land on these shores? The wording of the Constitution answers some of these questions, while the Bill of Rights answers the others. There is also the arena of human rights, which is supposed to supercede both in a globally connected world. Arab Americans and other immigrant-descended citizens are deploying both a local and a global narrative in their nascent press for civil rights.

Taking Professor Paik's warnings to heart, readers see that the denial of civil rights and liberties to Arab and Muslim Americans is not exceptional. It is another instance of exclusion from the democracy promised in a long line over a long time. Professor Maira asserts that linking protests of Arab Americans to black and other civil rights struggles de-exceptionalizes it and in many ways legitimatizes it. The persecution of "suspect populations" since 9/11 has created a framework into which they can put their angst. Though the array of advocacy for civil rights and liberties for Arab Americans is small, their persistence in building alliances makes for a large voice. A brief review of some of their current work is informative. Arab Muslims and Christians have joined hands in many of these endeavors.

The governing board of the ACLU elected its first Arab American in 2009, a move that perhaps underscored the widespread concern about the civil rights of Arab Americans post–9/11. "It is very important for the Arab American community to have our concerns heard," said Laila Qatami, the ACLU's new board member. "When we are able to help guide the legislative agenda for an organization like the ACLU, it is a very big milestone" ("ACLU Elects First Arab-American").

Another organization, the Arab American Civil Rights League, was founded in 2011 and is a nonprofit organization committed to protecting the civil rights of Arab Americans through education and advocacy.

American-Arab Anti-Discrimination Committee Support for Efforts to Stop Illegal Spying

The American-Arab Anti-Discrimination Committee (ADC) was one of several civil rights organizations that submitted a friend of the court brief in the case *American Civil Liberties Union v. National Security Agency* (2007), a case related to the National Security Agency's domestic spying and wiretapping programs, under which the agency intercepted international telephone and Internet communications without a court order. The ADC was joined in the amicus brief by the National Association for the Advancement of Colored People, the Asian American Legal Defense and Education Fund, United for Peace and Justice, and the Japanese American Citizens League.

In the past, the ADC voiced concerns about the U.S. government's surveillance practices that infringe on the civil rights and liberties of Americans and sidestep the system of checks and balances. In particular, the ADC feels that these practices create an environment of mistrust and apprehension for Arab Americans, who may now be afraid to communicate with family members in the Middle East because their conversations may be misunderstood or mistranslated by the National Security Agency or other federal agencies with access to this information.

Another organization, the Muslim Public Affairs Council (MPAC), upholds constitutional values to preserve liberty, equality, and justice for all. The organization works with a wide variety of public officials and civil rights and community organizations to protect the civil rights of all Americans.

The MPAC works with the Department of Justice's Civil Rights and Civil Liberties division on hate crime cases. In 2007, the Department of Justice prosecuted and convicted a person in federal court for charges related to threats made to a Muslim woman. The MPAC is the only Muslim American organization represented at the interagency meeting hosted by the Department of Justice that brings together community organizations with the Department of Homeland Security and the Treasury Department. The Workplace Religious Freedom Act and the End Racial Profiling Act are among the key pieces of legislation that the MPAC has worked to pass.

Most advocates for civil liberties reside on the leftist half of the political spectrum and have formed a network, Discover the Networks. The website (discoverthenetworks.org) provides a wealth of information for researchers on this topic.

The major organizations in America's contemporary civil liberties establishment include, among others, the Center for Constitutional Rights, the ACLU, the Bill of Rights Defense Committee, and the National Lawyers Guild. These groups share an ideological framework that casts the U.S. government as an "oppressive" regime at home and an imperialist intruder overseas; depicts America as a nation that discriminates heavily against designated "victim" groups such as nonwhites, women, homosexuals, Muslims, and people with disabilities; and violates the civil liberties of terrorist and criminal suspects in the name of public safety and homeland security. Similar perspectives are also held by such Muslim advocacy organizations as the American Muslim Alliance, the American Muslim Council, the ADC, the Council on American-Islamic Relations, the Islamic Circle of North America, the Islamic Society of North America, the Muslim American Society, the MPAC, and the Muslim Students Association of the United States and Canada.

One challenge for some young adults is the notion of inclusion. To what kind of society do they wish to be included? Do they want to join the status quo, which excludes based on race, color, and class, or do they want to assist in the creation of a society that lives more fully up to its democratic promises? How are they going to be better at the process of inclusion? How are they going to mediate—or are they going to try to mediate—decades-old conflicts that occupy the minds and hearts of the Arab and Muslim community? If the presence of an American Jew on a political ticket makes significant numbers of Arabs abandon their political party of choice, how are they going to reconcile living in a multireligious, multiethnic, multiracial society?

Maira interviewed some of these young adults and found a much more radical take on the issues. Whereas many civil rights movements are considered complete with the result of inclusion in the American experiment with democracy, others see a more realistic side, one of ongoing repression with periodic symbolic offerings of pacification. One interviewee saw just these things and called for an outing of those forces who initiated and carried out repressions, along with a different kind of commitment on the part of those who truly wished to participate in the struggle for civil rights and liberties.

These analyses, Maira suggested (and many agree), go beyond critique of the local to seeing global connections. Hip-hop music is one tool for making these connections real. Though music is one heartbeat of the Arab world along with poetry and prose, many older Arabs Americans and especially practicing Muslims have attempted to downplay its importance. Their children and grandchildren, however, are wading through the learned rejection in some cases and ambivalence in other cases to connect with their overseas and at-home counterparts.

The internal policing and surveillance of young adult Arabs and Muslims by the elders has long outlived its practical usefulness but still serves to temper outright appreciation of some for the creative impulses. Gossip often carries back to religious or home camps the stories of youths observed at gatherings where music is part of the menu, along with the potential for being labeled a rebel or worse.

In 2006, Belief Net stepped into this conversation on Arab and Muslim hip-hop:

> They rap about checkpoints, military oppression, and refugee camps. Their songs express longing for Jerusalem and anger at the hardships of life in the Gaza Strip and West Bank. But they grew up in Tennessee or Virginia, live in Los Angeles, and perform in New York City. Far away from their parents' homeland in the Middle East, Arab American rappers are trying to find their own voice in the United States—expressing the frustration of the [Arab and] Muslim world at a time when anti-Muslim feelings are on the rise following the Sept. 11 attacks. ("Halal Hip-Hop" 2006).

Hip-hop is a genre of music developed in the United States by inner-city African Americans in the 1970s. It consists of stylized rhythmic music accompanying prose that is mostly spoken. The basic instruments are voice, a drum box, and a turntable. As a genre that expresses or frames the black experience of repression, anxiety about police brutality, and violence in general, it also can be misogynist. Its social themes, however, remain the tour de force. It is this expression that has attracted some talented Arab and Muslim youths.

New Strategies of Activism

As 9/11 generations mature and learn to sift through their social, political, and economic seating both locally and globally, they have to stay within the home culture and simultaneously strike out for new vistas. For the past 17 years, Arab Americans have lived under unrelenting scrutiny, surveillance, and suspicion. Their children have grown up with strained identities, shamed names, and shamed and suspicious language. These children are bullied and diminished with each new assault on their being.

The first generation of Arab immigrants to live in America in the early 20th century largely assimilated, changed or morphed their names, and settled in to live the American Dream. When the world was not at war, they could send money home to secure family holdings there. They could bring family members to the United States if they wanted to come. Their numbers were insignificant in the thousands of immigrants at the time, and thus they could become invisible.

Arab immigrants were simultaneously surrounded by an invisible set of perceptions that were held over from Christianity and Europe's encounter with Islam and Muslims. As the Christian Church broke into Western and Eastern churches (with Eastern churches establishing themselves in eastern regions among ethnic groups), Arab Christians became an undeniable entity. They shared culture later designated as Middle Eastern/Arab Muslim. When pitted against other ethnicities, they are Arabs.

The Arab-Israeli wars rocked the psyches of Arab Americans. These invisible people realized that they had no voice in the lobbies in Washington, D.C., and no history with the American people to make a case for their stories of displacement. The very invisibility that aided in a reasonably smooth settlement now held the seeds of discontent. The land that held out the promise of democracy, civil rights, and liberties could not be enjoined in the fight to preserve even human dignity in the homeland.

As the Middle Eastern conflicts began to multiply, the issues of Palestinian Christians and Muslims took center stage. All Arabs became defined and defined themselves to some extent by the ongoing Arab-Israeli conflict. All Arabs became Palestinian to one degree or another, with their individual national and cultural identities submerged. To other Americans, citizens of all 22 Arab countries were molded into a monolith with only one problem—Israelis in particular and Jews in general.

The Arab oil embargo did little to flesh out distinctions between Arabs, nor did it endear other Americans to any cause. The caricatures of Arabs in the movies became real in the political cartoons of the 1970s and 1980s. Simultaneously, American universities and colleges began to teach Middle Eastern studies, fully supported by the government. Scores of graduate programs sprang up at the best schools and taught linguists, anthropologists, sociologists, and historians. These young scholars formed the foundation for scores of specialties. The only aspect missing to provide legitimacy for the effort was the recruitment of actual Arabs.

Many scholars sought to make sense of the 22 countries that comprise the Middle East, despite the political winds that constantly blew. Their limited understandings of the cultures involved and their differences, along with the political and religious biases of the Arabs hired to provide legitimacy, relegated the Middle East to the realms of the unknowable. The mysteriousness and exoticism portrayed in the movies was again dragged from the memory vault of the American public. The land of sensual dancing girls, licentious men, and sand—the usual motifs—now became the pictures on academic book covers.

The differences and similarities in the roots of Arab Christians, Muslims, and religious others largely revolve around religion, not culture, and national home, not language, quality, or kind of conflict. While readers may now in the 21st century think that the roots of conflict lie in religious controversy, that is a later development. A rise in religious sentiment from Muslim quarters and the takeover of control of al-Aqsa Mosque (Islam's third-holiest site) turned a political set of outrages with religious takeovers and controversies into a religious one, full blown.

Casting the religious State of Israel as the island of democracy and liberty in a sea of despotism and chaos has only fueled flames of hostility. These hostilities have flowed from the Middle East to America constantly. Even assertions of femininity have suffered under the bright lights of oppression of women. Arab American women's experience of women's suffrage paralleled if not preceded that of American women, and its continuation has been unbroken. Nevertheless, as all Arab American women came to be subsumed under the category "oppressed Arab Muslim women," a long history was overshadowed.

In the United States, a natural comparison can be made between Arab American women and women in other minority religious and ethnic groups because of size and perhaps conservative values. This, however, is where much of the comparison ends. Arab women are subject to a history that dates back more than 100 years and a contemporary existence mired in conflict and suspicion. All immigrants seek to maintain the language and culture of the homeland, and mothers teach much of this. As reservoirs of culture and language transmission, mothers play an almost irreplaceable role in the family, which does not necessarily prevent them from pursuing their own self-interests. In many minority religious communities in the United States, women's self-interests are in total alignment with the home. This has not been the case with many Arab women. Just living in the United States has nonetheless challenged their task.

Organizations such as Arab American Family Services shows that the particular needs of Arab American families, only tangentially addressed in mainstream services, can marry the civic service ambitions of women with the need to serve families:

> Arab American Family Services (AAFS), a nonprofit social service agency founded in 2001, provides caring, compassionate assistance to (South Suburban) Chicagoland residents, with special sensitivity to the cultural and linguistic needs of Arab Americans. AAFS offers support in the areas of public benefits, immigration, domestic violence, mental health, and elderly services and sponsors outreach programs to build healthier families and communities. As a locally focused, nonpolitical and nonreligious agency, AAFS takes a leading role in building bridges, respect and understanding between Arab-American and mainstream-American cultures. ("About Us")

On the website medium.com, an Arab Christian woman tells another story of dealing with the intricacies of America's racial hierarchy rather than oppression:

> I remember the first time I had to decide which box to check under "Race/Ethnicity" on an official form. I was sitting for my PSATs during my sophomore year of high school, and those empty boxes were severely escalating my present state of anxiety. I checked "Other", erased it, and then checked "White". If I checked "Other." I would have to specify and I couldn't think of an existing word to describe my race. In that moment I felt invisible. (Jahchan 2016)

Being white in skin tone—but Mediterranean white, not European white—has been a problem for Arab American families, especially since skin tones may vary inside families. The social construction of race continues to influence Arab American identity in unprecedented ways. Language accents prevent some from passing as white, while skin tones betray others. Some Arabs consider themselves African, while others, such as Egyptians, live in a nether region—not African and not European. Checking the right box causes reflection but also has consequences.

In the United States, the box can enhance privileges or deny them. It can assist in getting into college or move a potential student out of the running for an affirmative action seat. Checking the right box can cause other consternations. The "right" box (white) can open up housing or prevent much-needed social services. Since the founding of this country, whiteness has been a privilege. The first Arab immigrants fought to be recognized as white, while some of their grandchildren struggle to fit into the resistances of the brown and black ghettos.

Professor Su'ad Abdul Khabeer explored this conundrum in her book *Muslim Cool:* "U.S. Muslim engagements with music reflect the dominant discourse on Blackness in the United States today" (Abdul Khabeer 2016, 79). Though many African Americans welcome Arabs to urban spaces, there is resistance to the claims being made about their presence. African Americans have witnessed many ethnicities, and even some in the dominant ethnicity gain "street credentials" along with a foothold on the American Dream in their midst. Being "cool" without struggle is the new and often recurring fashion statement. For the black community, ethnicities come, get what they need for their conscience and consciousness, and then go, having had an experience of being close to the rejected of society, all without any pain.

Abdul Kabeer goes on to memorialize what has been made of the hood in hip-hop and rap music as the Arab experiment continues. Hip-hop serves to connect Arab American youths to Arab youths everywhere. In the global dimension, more Arab nationalist tones and language take over, as lyrics are in Arabic, not English. Increasingly, to keep feelings among those who know the angst, in America the lyrics are Arabic. A new hood formed. Parents and grandparents are threatened by forays into the hood and the ideas about resistance brought from there. As young adults become more Americanized, all efforts are made to reintroduce them to Arab culture.

Observed in April, Arab American Heritage Month is a time to reflect on the contributions of Arab Americans and the diverse group of people who make up the nation's Middle Eastern population. Every year the theme has changed, but the duality of pride in Arabness and Americanness remains.

At the Smithsonian Institution Archives, the family of Dr. Alixa Naff deposited her interviews and photographs of Arab Americans who came to the United States between 1895 and World War II. This collection at the Smithsonian has become a favored visiting place for Arab Americans during celebrations of Arab American history. Other larger collections are on display in Dearborn's Arab American Museum.

Profiles

Alixa Naff (1919–2013) was a Lebanese-born American historian who focused much of her research on Arab immigration to the United States in the 20th century. She documented Arab immigration to the United States during the late 19th and early 20th centuries, and her research and artifact collection is on display at the Smithsonian Institution in Washington, D.C.

Rami Nashshibi (n.d.–) is a Chicago-based activist-organizer who was born in Amman, Jordan. From a secular cosmopolitan family who lived in Romania, Spain, Saudi Arabia, and Italy, he settled in Chicago. Cofounding IMAN, Nashshibi moved to establish in Chicago's southwest side a holistic center serving the community. The work of IMAN is nationally and internationally known for its many programs.

Zaher Sahloul (n.d.–) is president of the Syrian American Medical Society, one of the leading medical relief organizations that serve the health care needs of Syrians during the ongoing humanitarian crisis. Dr. Sahloul, originally from Homs, Syria, is a practicing critical care specialist at Christ Advocate Medical Center in Chicago. Recently he completed a medical mission in the northern Syrian city of Aleppo, where he closely reviewed the medical and humanitarian situation on the ground. He has completed several other medical missions in Syria, Jordan, Turkey, Lebanon, and Iraq in the past three years. Sahloul has helped train medical relief workers in topics such as medical practice in war zones, dealing with limited resources, and disaster management.

References

Abdul Khabeer, Su'ad. *Muslim Cool: Race, Religion, and Hip Hop in the United States.* New York: New York University Press, 2016.

"About Us." Arab American Family Services, arabamericanfamilyservices.org /about-us/.

"ACLU Elects First Arab-American." Voice of America, October 31, 2009, https://www.voanews.com/a/a-13-2006-11-15-voa43/314246.html.

Ariens, Michael A. *American Constitutional Law and History.* Durham, NC: Carolina Academic Press, 2012.

"Halal Hip-Hop: At a Time When Anti-Islamic Feelings Are on the Rise, Some Muslim and Arab-American Rappers Are Finding a Voice in the U.S." Belief Net, April 3, 2006, http://www.beliefnet.com/entertainment/music /2006/04/halal-hip-hop.aspx.

Jahchan, Chantal. "On Being a Christian Arab-American Woman in America." Medium, August 1, 2016, https://medium.com/@chantaljahchan/what -its-like-to-be-a-christian-arab-american-woman-in-america-f3886 1405c99.

Paik, A. Naomi. *Rightlessness: Testimony and Redress in U.S. Prison Camps since World War II.* Chapel Hill: University of North Carolina Press, 2016.

Sirin, Selcuk R., and Michelle Fine. *Muslim American Youth: Understanding Hyphenated Identities through Multiple Methods.* New York: New York University Press, 2008.

CHAPTER SIX

Women

Anchors of Community

Upon arriving in America, many Arab Christian women found that they and their families were finally free from Muslim rule and its subjugations. They quickly formed women's organizations to assist in resettlement in the United States. Initially, they too created traditions that included analyses of that subjugation for subsequent generations. Depending on the fate of the family under Ottoman rule, the analysis of their prior subjugation was told as either relief from the way it was or as unparalleled hatred of Islam and Muslims. The few Arab Muslim women who migrated came in the beginning of the 20th century. While most Arab Christian women lived in ethnic enclaves at the beginning of the 20th century, their interactions with American society were influential. When Arab Muslim women came in the middle of the 20th century they also lived in ethnic enclaves, but their interactions with American society were minimal.

This chapter will explore Arab American women as minority religious women in the context of religious women of other minorities living virtually and totally isolated lives in some instances and partially integrated lives in other instances. It will also examine their cultural lives as they have transported them to America.

Context

As with many other immigrant groups, language, religion, class, and region of origin determined a great deal about the character of the U.S. Arab community. Enclaves of women knew and still know the town and

An Arab American community in New York, dubbed "The Syrian Colony" in 1916. (Library of Congress)

sometimes the precise village where their neighbors originated. In both Christian and Muslim groups, traditional values, behaviors, and attitudes were and are upheld as the only acceptable comportment. Among many Muslim women these acceptable comportments are not left to individual accountability, since communities use several tools for surveillance of women. Old world and now new world policing involves gossip, threats of slander, and even violent discipline. This environment envelops the lives of community members.

When investigating ethnic, religious, or even same-language communities, the terms "traditional," "liberal," "conservative," and "secular" are often used without definition. The term "traditional" refers in a positive way to long-established values, from the simple covering of one's mouth during a sneeze to cooking from a long-held family recipe to having an annual family reunion. The term "liberal," on the other hand, signals openness to a new behavior or opinion while discarding the long-established behavior or opinion. For example, today families sometimes text on cell phones or take phone calls during dinnertime, disregarding the long-established behavior of reserving dinnertime for family talk. The term "conservative" incorporates the term "traditional" in that it holds to tradition regarding politics or religion. "Secular" is the broadest of the terms in that it refers to attitudes or activities that are not based in religion or spirituality. Perhaps what is crucial to add here is the term "created traditions."

Created traditions are those that valorize cultural traditions in the face of attempts to "count" in an increasingly global context. Globalization has been somewhat successful not in promoting multicultural exchanges but instead in forcing protections of cultural identity and the formation of hypercultural existences. In cultures, traditions become codified as the way it has always been. What is neglected in this narration is the fact that many ways of doing things were tried and tested, and some were rejected, modified, and retested over time. Those ways of doing things that survived scrutiny and testing became the foundation of tradition. As long as communities were relatively isolated or existed next to communities that had similar traditions, the maintenance of tradition was relatively easy.

Migration

Many Arab women migrated to join husbands in either the tenements of urban spaces before the 1980s or lower-class and lower-middle-class neighborhoods after the 1980s. These are comparably tightly packed spaces full of strangers. Apartments and houses are close to each other, some with windows into each other's living spaces. In the ancestral land, homes are arranged to accommodate the public and the private inside the home. The family spaces are generally hidden from the space to entertain strangers. Women in a family are accustomed to their private space, where they gather outside of the gaze of men. Friendly and accessible butchers, bakers, and produce farmers are also nonexistent. Reworking how to plan for a new way of household living is largely a task for women. Traditions had to be re-created to fit a new environment.

Understanding re-created traditions is important in understanding what happens in the cycles of migration. People migrate for a variety of reasons. For many there are multiple migrations to an ultimate destination, voluntarily or involuntarily, and traditions are re-created with each migration. Homesickness causes every migrant to reimagine home in a pristine and loving way. In the 20th century, the Middle East was rapidly changing; clinging to traditions of cooking, cleaning, and arranging households felt necessary. Perhaps the changes were not as visible as the industrial changes in the West, but modern technologies found their way to the Middle East and provided conveniences or longing in the same ways. Women understood themselves in one of two ways: those who were led to re-create traditions (which sometimes evolved into hyperexpressions) and those for whom migration presented an opportunity to create a new identity.

Different Identities

Arab Christian women comprised small numbers of early immigrant arrivals. Culturally they were similar to the Muslim women of the region.

Immigrant inspectors assumed this similarity at the beginning of the 20th century and denied citizenship on these grounds, forcing applicants to prove that they were Christian.

Many Arab Christian women found educational opportunities and furthered or gained skills, which led second and third generations to fruitful employment when desired. Most Arab Muslim women who came to the United States during the 1980s and 1990s (after wars between Israel and Palestine) were Palestinian and Syrian, though there were Egyptians and Jordanians. Because of this forced dislocation, they immediately begin to re-create an imagined prior peaceful living in various enclaves across the country. There was also a difference in social economic status of Arab migrants; many Syrians were professionals (such as doctors, engineers, and architects), while many Palestinians were small businessmen and entrepreneurs. Socioeconomic class determined where they lived and thus their experience of America.

In the United States, the re-creation of an imagined community evolved also into a hyperexpression of Islam. These reimagined communities became conservative religious enclaves separate from much of American society. They resemble small European American conservative religious communities, which also evolved into hyperexpressions of particular understandings of Christianity. The most familiar of these communities are the Amish, the Mennonites, and the Mormons.

Small Religious Communities in the United States

The United States became home to quite a few small European-originated Protestant communities as early as the 18th century and home to an American-created religion in the early 19th century. Many of these groups were Germanic and spoke specific German dialects, which were incorporated into their worship services and everyday communications. Mennonites, Amish, and Mormons lived separately from the larger society in an effort to maintain their distance from contamination by secular society. These communities also created hypercultural existences with little social contact with majority religious communities or the social life surrounding them; they lived in bubbles.

These bubbles multiplied, however, with groups such as the Jehovah's Witnesses, who took their challenges of religious freedom to court. Mennonites and Amish live mostly in semirural and rural areas. Mormons, on the other hand, have become urban and political. Jehovah's Witnesses have a public proselytization ministry in urban and rural areas. Only the Mormons and Jehovah's Witnesses proselytize. Nevertheless, their family structures and roles of women are most appropriate for comparison to the small groups of Arab Muslim women.

Women in Small Religious Communities

In three centuries, little has changed regarding language except that rudimentary English has been added for selling in the marketplaces. Globalization forced the creation of impenetrable bubbles of existence in multicultural societies. Women as the anchors of families and thus communities are the repositories of tradition inside of those bubbles. For the purpose of this text, a view of religiously conservative women, such as those in Amish and Mennonite communities, is appropriate. They belong to a minority religiously conservative community that in many ways resembles some of the Arab communities.

Women in the most traditionally conservative religious communities such as the Old Order Amish and Mennonites in America adhere to the customs brought over three centuries ago called "plainness" in regard to dress and appearance as a mark of modesty. Women in Mormon, Mennonite, and Amish communities typically wear unadorned dress. The high political office held by Mitt Romney required that his wife's dresses be a little more fashionable, but they were still unadorned and unrevealing. Female members of Jehovah's Witnesses communities dress stylishly but are very reserved in their manner even while proselytizing.

In Amish or Mennonite communities, hard work is preferred to convenience, and many work without electricity or telephones in their homes. Their work as mothers, home managers, religious women, and active community members is highly valued by both women and men in the community. There is communal awareness that individuals have their own interests and that self-interests are normal; care is given to weave them into the self-interests of the family and community. High intelligence is valued, and handicaps are seen as gifts from God, but particular attention is not placed on these individuals who must continue to work in the community. Overall, there is a suspicion of secular society and its endeavors that lead one away from worship of God. This perception keeps contact with the larger society minimal.

Education

Secular education is valued only in its most basic forms of reading, writing, and arithmetic in Amish communities. Beyond the educational basics, learning is religious and pragmatic, focusing on vocational skills and homemaking. This "plain" existence harms nothing and no one, and members of the community live in tune with the ecosystem. Women do not consider themselves oppressed, nor are they spoken of as oppressed in the few existing studies. Though the Amish use few if any public utilities and do not acquire the debt that other Americans do, the federal government taxes them as usual (with the exception of social security).

Other small religious communities generally put effort into the education of their young men, though young women are increasingly enrolled in college especially from the Arab community. Some first-generation Arab women, both Christian and Muslim, see education as a stepping-stone for professional lives in journalism, medicine, law, and various nonprofit organizations. They are teaching their daughters a new Arab identity while maintaining some traditions (including family honor) especially in choice of mates. Interestingly, there is evidence of marriage across ethnic, religious, and racial boundaries. While these marriages are highly contested and sometimes accompanied by disinheritance and violence, they are still occurring. Some researchers assert that this is a direct result of the diversity present in colleges.

If women go to university, it is preferable that they stay at home, attending nearby schools. This arrangement keeps their social circle small and is designed to limit their social contact with non-Arab males. Conservative families also prohibit any attendance at school events as well as sorority membership and work-study employment. Many colleges are now requiring service learning, and this is proving to be problematic for both the young women and their families. Many of these service learning programs require participation in communities around cities, where the potential for negative influences (such as contact with non-Arab men and women) is too high. This is not unlike the fears of those in the Amish, Mennonite, and Mormon communities. Although the Mormon and Jehovah's Witnesses communities proselytize, their young people are severely cautioned to have no contact outside of spreading the word.

There is at least one Christian Arab American women's organization that mentors women in professions and careers, the Arab American Women's Business Council. Women are mentored in skills such as negotiation, résumé writing, investing, and business marketing. The council hopes to have an online educational program up and running soon. Meanwhile, the council sponsors a limited number of scholarships for Arab American women to assist in attending college. Christian Arab women are not under the same religious strictures as their Muslim counterparts and have been able to take advantage of the opportunities offered them in the United States. The council has extended a hand to Muslim women who are able to take advantage of these opportunities and have subsequently joined.

The National Arab American Women's Association is a warehouse of information regarding events. Its mission is to provide self-empowerment, individual freedom, human dignity, community outreach, and cultural investment. Overall, it seeks to act as a bridge to bring together the diverse Arab American community, Christian and Muslim. Women who are housewives may also work in the family business or work a part-time or full-time job elsewhere. Like other American women, they balance work and family obligations. They are fashion designers, models, journalists, entertainers, professors, and politicians.

Using the context of women in small ethnic, linguistic, and religious communities is critical for a brief discussion of Arab American women's understanding of their national ethnic identity. Arab American women have been categorized as an ethnic group that originates from at least 17 countries and are classified by the census (and generally classify themselves) as non-Hispanic whites. In reality, they are Christian and Muslim women from 22 countries with various cultural and racial identities.

The majority of American-born Arab women are descendants and family members of Orthodox Arab Christians who migrated beginning in the last decade of the 19th century. Arab Americans at that time constituted a minuscule portion of immigrant rosters of ships, and almost all came from the Ottoman Empire region then called Greater Syria. In Muslim communities, there is more focus on traditional values of family: chastity for young women, young marriages, and religious and culturally inspired dress. Educated Arab Christian women have largely been successful in the United States as educators, businesswomen, and other professionals. Nevertheless, almost all in these communities see traditional values as being worth preservation and establish supertraditional versions of them.

Family is the centerpiece of community life. Family consults, eats together, depends on one another for status, discusses most major decisions, and is especially dominant in discussions of marriage. Family size varies. Some Arabs are invested in large families, while others have only one or two children. Inside these microsocieties, families have status to maintain, especially in Muslim communities. The burden of family honor falls on women.

Transnational Connections versus Civil Life

Unlike minority religious communities who migrated in order to flee religious persecution in the 18th century, Arab American women are truly

An image from Arab-American Heritage Week, 2010. (Robert Nickelsberg/Getty Images)

transnational. They travel with relative frequency to the ancestral home and the homes of family members who migrated elsewhere. For many women the United States is just one home, as family is spread among several Western countries in addition to the area of origin. While groups such as the Amish and the Mennonites see themselves as American (though "old world" and very conservative religiously), almost all Americans of Arab descent define themselves as Arab first. Global politics does not influence them, nor does it determine their American status. They are not in fear of deportation or police surveillance.

Participation in the civic life of a democracy is largely lost, especially for Arab Muslim women. Traditional life, including gender roles, militates against even minimal levels of political awareness beyond Middle Eastern politics and U.S. involvement in them. There are attempts by immigrant families to keep second-generation women close to family and socialized into Middle Eastern rather than American society. Families are not in favor of professional education, as that status decreases opportunities for marriage inside the community. Nevertheless, young Arab American women find themselves increasingly involved in the sociopolitical spaces of

America in protests around refugees and associated issues and are testing the waters of involvement in U.S. politics, much to the chagrin of families and communities. In the hypercultural expression, interactions with men of all religions and ethnicities are still frowned upon, as is too much public involvement.

Absence from civic engagement means absence from discussion of topics such as abortion and sexual orientation. Arab Christian women tend to be more socialized as Americans, and though Arab mates of the same spiritual seating are preferred, non-Arab mates are not excluded from being possibilities. Some young women have begun to break with many of these hypercultural expressions by marrying men from other ethnic groups and moving away from the communities of their parents. Some families have threatened to cut them off from inheritances or never speak to them again, but as time goes by much is negotiated, as family ties remain strong.

Ethnic Difference

There is a linguistic and social hierarchy among Arabs, as in other racial/ethnic groups. Women play a decisive role in maintaining status. Skin color also plays a pivotal role. Syrian women marry Syrian men of equal or higher status, and Sudanese women marry Sudanese men as a first preference. Saudis generally marry Saudis. Nationality plays a role, as does place on the Arabic-language ladder. Allowances are made for wealth and power, of course. Some Arab men, however, have married American women to get green cards and then divorced them after citizenship was attained. Very recently, young Arab women have risked connections to family and inheritance to expand their marriage prospects to outside their national group but only on rare occasions outside their racial group.

Although women in some ethnic minority religious communities initially suffered some religious persecution or isolation in the United States, the case of Arab Muslim women is as of yet unrelenting. This has at least twin causes—their self-initiated isolation and movies. The problem is one of dissonance at its best.

The Scarf and Surveillance

In the movies, whether silent or epic, Arab women were portrayed as anything but demure, shy, or pious. The obviously Muslim Arab women (and "obviously" is the operative word, since most Arab women are indistinguishable from other white women) is one cause of threat and discrimination. The few Arab Muslim women who wear scarves stand out precisely because of their scarves. Observers know that they are not nuns because of the colorfulness of the clothing and do not attach piety because Arab Muslim women are not Amish, other plain-dressed women, or nuns. Yet, they certainly do not resemble what is seen in movies. The exceptions are news reports of similarly dressed Arab women who are seen with AK-47s being trained for war in various Arab countries.

The movie *True Lies* (1994) introduced American audiences to a new Arab woman stereotyped as an AK-47-wielding gun moll who is as treacherous as her male counterpart. In this film, a female terrorist is introduced as a treacherous woman who displays malice and hatred toward the American travelers on an airplane. She is ready to hurt and kill. Tashfeen Malik, one of the terrorists in the San Bernardino, California, attack on 37 of her husband's coworkers, reinforced this image more than a decade later. Even though Malik was Pakistani, her Arab style of dress associated her with the already assumed terrorist nature of Muslims. The traditional religious dress of some Muslim women is now transformed into the equivalent of the knapsack as concealment for weapons. Investigative reporters immediately found that about 10 percent of Muslims joining the Islamic State of Iraq and Syria (ISIS) are women, and more than 14 percent of Americans captured for joining ISIS or plotting ISIS-inspired attacks are women.

After San Bernardino, the *hijab* is no longer viewed by authorities as a quaint anachronism or symbol of modesty. It is now a real potential sign of threat or as passive terrorism and an indication of radicalization. American movies depicted Arab women as beautiful, veiled, cunning, and sly but only threatening in affairs of the heart. Now the United States had firsthand evidence of some veiled Arab Muslim women not only assisting male terrorists but also acting as terrorists themselves.

Women are the repositories of family reputation. Community gossip, innuendo, and now cybergossip form an almost invisible boundary of internal surveillance around significant numbers of women's choices to wear or not wear a head scarf. Externally, they are surveilled by U.S. security forces as potential supporters or actors of terrorism because of the scarf. Their families come under surveillance due to the associations young women keep. Because families are close-knit and social circles are small, women have a hyperawareness of their actions and speech. All Arab women know the value of a good reputation and the woes of a suspect reputation. The increased surveillance from inside and outside on the lives of young women has created a great deal of angst. Some young women have begun to burst through the strictures.

Just as there are always conflations of a wide diversity for ease of refer-ences and conversations, this case is no different. Muslim women, primar-ily those who veil, dominate a complicated public and private discourse in America. The public discourses include legal issues such as discrimina-tion/harassment, public harassment by strangers and law enforcement, and girls in schools and sports seeking to change rules to accommodate their dress. Scholars and researchers have interviewed women and popu-larized their analyses of answers. Politicians have commented publicly on the dress of Muslim women. Private discourses that occur in families and communities often refer to an obligation for pious Muslim women to veil and cover their bodies in a particular way. Conservative families and indi-viduals understand veiling to be demanded by God.

Public and Private Religion

The history of Arab Muslim women was an imagined one long before their actual physical presence in perceivable numbers in the United States. Arab women were portrayed as exotic, tantalizing, highly sexual, and thinly veiled women whom men must control. They were portrayed as quietly lusting after any man with money or status. Women in other small religiously conservative communities did not have an imagined persona that preceded them and their immigration to America, and thus this is one place where much of the comparison is not appropriate.

In the United States, the distinction between public and religious affairs is paramount. Most apparent in public spaces is the need for means of identification and that one religious faith should not have undue power over all others. For example, public schools do not permit the wearing of religious garb that indicates religious authority, such as a nun's habit. In a multicultural, multireligious society that already had a Protestant Chris-tian foundation, this separation assuredly was to prevent the domination of one denomination. Later it provided a relatively reasonable space for all religious citizens to enjoy their First Amendment rights. Protestants had fled Catholic domination and wanted to avoid a repeat of religious rule. This attitude was further expressed in an initial harassment of Catholics and their subsequent formation of a private school system. This pattern of religious expression is open to all.

This system enabled Amish, Mennonites, and Mormons to set up their internal religious systems and, beyond compulsory education, make deci-sions about other interactions with the larger society. Young people were taught what the religious community felt they needed to know, with no interference from the government. For those Mormons and Jehovah's

Witnesses who worked in the larger society, some social aspects of employment were and still are negotiated. For example, Mormons do not drink alcohol and need to negotiate to not be seen as noncollegial. The history of religions in America is a history of negotiations. But none of those negotiations can supersede the emphasis on secularism.

Feminist Awakenings

Arab women immigrants arrived to a society that had some freedoms for pioneering women but few for urban women. American women only won the vote after decades of the suffrage movement, and this privilege was not without its public detractors. Immigrant women, many of whom did not speak English, would not have immediately benefited from any aspects of the suffrage movement in the United States. Those Arab women who came from Egypt, however, would have been familiar with the struggles of women for rights. As in the United States, upper-middle-class women usually led suffrage movements in Egypt, which included a strong literary component and demands for political empowerment.

As mentioned earlier, middle-class women, both Christian and Muslim, began coming to the United States in the 1980s after wars with the State of Israel and would have been aware of the "feminist awakening" and its subsequent movements in the latter half of the 20th and 21st centuries. Needless to say, few would have been initially aware of the movies about them or that those visual images had formed lasting opinions. All were aware of the European fascination with the harem, which was evident in literary and artistic productions. Conflicts in the Middle East obscured much real scholarly discussion of any potential plight of Arab women until Elizabeth Fernea's *Guests of the Sheikh* was published in 1965. This ethnographic study of the women in a small village in Iraq became a modern look at Muslim women in the Muslim world.

Ethnographies of Arab women in the Middle East began to appear in American college and university syllabi, and those images and attitudes were superimposed on Arab immigrant women in America without any mention of an inheritance of feminism. Women in villages and towns who veiled became the norm for all Arab women everywhere. Most Americans did not distinguish the Christians from the Muslims, since all were culturally the same or at least potentially the same. They were backward and undereducated if educated at all and destined to be married early.

The other significant external factor highly influential in the creation of the hypercultural religious expression was the effort of the authorities in Saudi Arabia to spread their very conservative understanding of

Islamic textual sources. Young and middle-aged men were taught in Saudi Arabia in the second half of the 20th century and then subsidized to act as imams or Islamic teachers across the world and especially in the West. These imams and teachers redefined Muslim piety for Muslim communities all over the world. For women, their piety resided in their dress in obedience to their husbands. The Wahhabi movement of Saudi Arabia removed many Arabs from public spaces, such as television anchors and news reporters.

Saudi-trained men claimed a legacy of Islamic education and all the authority that conferred. They taught an austere Islamic practice in which women were to be totally separated from men and to dress as close to the covering of a Saudi woman's dress as possible. A long, loose trench coat in gray, black, or brown became the norm in America for year-round wear. Women were to wear socks when outside the home, as men should not see their feet. Husbands, fathers, and sons and subsequently women demanded this particular dress and attitude as the only acceptable mark of modesty and piety and thus religion. Religious women were seen in public spaces initially and later, when permitted, inside of designated mosque spaces. This is one mark of hypercultural religious expression. Before the intrusion of Saudi Arabian Islamic understandings into their lives, the numbers of Arab women who covered their heads varied with education, social economic status, and colonial/global experiences. An assessment of whether or not they were pious was not mentioned amid interviews of adult women in the 1970s.

Arab American women from families who did not veil usually recounted negative interactions with religious authority under repressive Muslim regimes. They had little response to the equation of veils with piety or religiosity beyond disgust. The demands of veiling for internal social belonging caused significant tensions in homes that were secular and those where the hypercultural religious expression was not present. Young men generally bowed to conservative family demands that they marry veiled women. The pressure of social and religious community belonging increased in the latter decades of the 20th century. For young women in a minority ethnic religious community, social inclusion is a high-priority item. While this complicated set of internal politics has proven thorny for women across generations, a few of them have not let the issue prevent their social activism.

Palestinian mothers who came in the second half of the 20th century spent a great deal of their time learning the ways of American society, shielding their children from what they did not understand and worrying about loved ones and land in the old country. As an ethnic minority, one focus was on supporting the procurement of places of worship. Although women were not used to attending the prayers in the mosque, it was assumed by the men that they would contribute to the building of the mosque. Soon Palestinian mothers found themselves joined with women from other Arab cultures. As the numbers of Arab women from other cultures grew, so too did the hypercultural religious expressions. The chastity and comportment of young Arab women became a focal point.

Marriage

Social events at the church or mosque, university, and family events provide opportunities for women to meet men. Generally speaking, parental permission and approval are sought for marriage even if the spouse is a relative. The tradition of arranged marriage is very much alive in conservative communities across the nation. All effort is put on making sure that these marriages survive. Increasingly, however, divorces are on the upswing.

For many, even traditional Muslim Arab Americans, a wedding consists of a license from city hall, the actual marriage ceremony, and the reception. The officials at city hall check as much as they can to make sure of eligibility for marriage. In some of these cases, they check to see if the man entered the United States on a spouse visa and when or if a divorce was registered. Some couples choose to get married in the parental home overseas so that family living there can attend, especially the elderly, and to skirt some American regulations regarding bigamy.

In Islam, according to the Qur'ān, women are entitled to a marriage contract, and it is this contract that validates the marriage. The purpose of the contract is to ensure the bride's consent to the marriage. It also enables the bride and the groom to have some guidelines for their relationship. For example, women can put in their contracts that they will continue their education or that there is a limit to the number of children they will bear. Contracts can also contain intentions about the care of elderly parents. In many ways, the contract is an opportunity for women to express what they consider a good marriage. For many American young Arab women, especially those who have migrated to the United States in recent decades, the marriage contract is reduced to consent. Women are encouraged to forgo their rights and just get married.

One of the rights under considerable debate is the *mahr,* an agreed-upon offering from the groom to the bride at the time of marriage. It can be a range of things, including jewelry, money, stocks and bonds, or even houses. Marriage in Islam is a contract and, like other contracts, can be broken, although every effort to maintain it is made. If the wife wants to break the contract and all other efforts fail, she can offer to return the *mahr* or some portion of it. The purpose of *mahr* is to give the bride some financial independence, so this offering should not be delayed; however, cultural innovations have given men the opportunity to promise this offering in the future, thereby obscuring its actual purpose. Women under pressure to marry have accepted this situation.

Divorce in Islam is permissible, but men have the upper hand religiously. They can easily perform a religious divorce by simply pronouncing it. The case of women religiously seeking divorce remains complicated. A civil divorce is required for issues of property settlement and child custody. Religious communities are not friendly to divorced women, and women do not wish to place themselves in the situation especially if they are reliant on the community for their social life. Nonreligious and liberal Arab women still face some scrutiny from communities if they are divorced.

Whiteness and Veils

Since most Arab Americans claim whiteness as their racial signification, discrimination against women is largely the same as with all American women in the workforce. The only distinctive discrimination is with Arab Muslim women who cover their heads as a sign of religious piety. This has caused complaints from coworkers and customers who feel as uncomfortable as they would with nuns or Amish women. Nevertheless, the presence of religion in the nonreligious workplace is troubling for many.

Arab American women's writings in fiction and nonfiction have generally focused on several themes in particular—body image, war, sex and sexual abuse, growing up between two cultures, and gender roles. The women's movement in the 1970s created an upsurge in the publication of women's literature and later in the writings of women of bicultural identities and women of color.

The writings of Arab American women often describe identity problems and the issues of living biculturally in a country where perceived cultural difference can result in death, harassment, or (for girls) sexual assault. The ancestral homes have the identical problems, and thus growing up is extremely difficult. There are difficulties in having unusual names, not attending social events, and experiencing family surveillance. Writers such as Mohja Kahf, Laila Halaby, and Diana Abu Jaber use fiction to narrate some of these sensitive stories. These writers have tackled issues of growing up in an American Muslim family that enshrouds Arab values without truly realizing that they live in America with sometimes conflicting ways.

The American story of Arab Americans includes post–9/11 fears, incorporating verbal and physical assaults on women, resistance to the current political climate with efforts to ban all but Christian Arabs, family members who are potentially prevented from coming into the country, U.S. family members being prevented from caring for the elderly elsewhere, and fears of deportation. Of course women and girls are scared.

Documentaries about Arabs and Arab women are being produced. As more women succeed in obtaining postgraduate degrees and get married while keeping their scarves on or off, they are providing role models for their peers and the next generation. The Women's March after the inauguration of U.S. president Donald Trump witnessed a number of Arab women featured as speakers and participants. Arab women, though still small in number, are beginning to make a presence.

Profiles

Yvonne Haddad (1935–) was born in Syria to a Maronite Christian family. She has been at the forefront of studies on Islam in America, often writing with Professor Jane Smith. Dr. Haddad has mentored countless young scholars in this field and in studies on the Middle East. Her most recent work is *A Vanishing Minority: Christians in the Middle East.*

Hoda Kotb (1964–) is an Arab American–born television personality of Egyptian descent and is viewed daily as a host of NBC's *Today Show.* Warm and charming, she provides the early-morning crowd with both hard news and trends across America. Kotb won a daytime Emmy in 2010.

Ilhan Oman (1982–) was born in Somalia and immigrated to the United States at age 12 after spending 4 years in a Kenyan refugee camp. She is the first Somali American Muslim woman elected to the state legislature in Minnesota.

Linda Sarsour (1980–) is an American-born activist of Palestinian descent. She began her activist work as a volunteer at the Arab American Association in New York City after 9/11. Sarsour fought with others to get Muslim holidays recognized in New York City public schools and has been a voice in the Black Lives Matter movement and women's leadership programs. She was a fellow at the New York University Robert F. Wagner Graduate School of Public Service.

References

Akhtar, Mohammad, and John Esposito. *Muslim Family in a Dilemma: Quest for a Western Identity*. Lanham, MD: University Press of America, 2006.

Haddad, Yvonne Y., and Jane Smith. *Muslim Women in America: The Challenge of Islamic Identity Today*. Oxford: Oxford University Press, 2011.

Halaby, Laila. *Once in a Promised Land*. New York: Beacon, 2007.

Kahf, Mohja. *The Girl in the Tangerine Scarf*. New York: Carroll and Graf, 2006.

MacFarlane, Julie. *Islamic Divorce in North America: A Shari'a Path in a Secular Society*. Oxford: Oxford University Press, 2012.

Stoltzfus, Louise. *Amish Women*. Brattleboro, VT: Good Books, 1997.

CHAPTER SEVEN

Representations of Arabs in American Media

In a speech in 2016 during the presidential campaign, Donald Trump asserted that he would ban Muslims from immigrating to the United States until immigration authorities could put in place a "more efficient vetting process." He also stated that those authorities should involve themselves in "extreme vetting" (Said-Moorhouse and Browne, 2016). Within a week of taking office he kept those campaign promises, though the targeted seven countries were not known as sources of terrorism against the United States. In fact, the countries of origin of known terrorists in the United States were not targeted, giving rise to speculation that President Trump's business and real estate holdings played a significant role in the decision. The targeted countries were almost all black African Muslim countries whose primary language was Arabic. Syrians were banned until further notice. This order remained stayed and was sent to the U.S. Supreme Court, which granted the government the right to continue with the ban.

The envisioning of Muslims as "other" that began in the 18th century in the literature of Protestant missionaries, diaries, and reports of captured statesmen such as Benjamin Franklin has been continued in almost every form of media into the 21st century. Coupled with the horrific attacks in the United States and around the world by those who are using the name of Islam as an ideological weapon to terrorize, a ban of some sort on Muslims becomes acceptable to large swaths of the American public. This chapter will present and explore the representations and stereotypes of Arab Americans in the late 20th and early 21st centuries.

Who Are Arab Americans in America?

Who are Arab Americans? They are not just the descendants of the Ottoman subjects at the beginning of the 20th century. They are not just the Arabs who fled Israeli control of their lands and the strife that followed. They have come from the various cultures of 22 countries. These cultures are bound by dialects of the same language and general mores (though of differing religious traditions). These countries all lived under Ottoman rule and suffered occupation under the rule of various European countries in the early 20th century. Their membership in the Ottoman Empire and subsequent European rule undoubtedly led to their being lumped together as "other" and not as distinct cultural or religious groups. Consequently, they have been melded into one of three stereotypes: oil sheikhs with excesses of money, wives, gold, sand, and turbans; beautiful women who are mysterious and sexually alluring; and poor, backward, uneducated or undereducated Palestinians who are fleeing to anywhere that will let them in. Finally, Arabs are seen as the only true Muslims.

Few if any of the Arabs who immigrated to the United States were sheikhs with enormous wealth. Those with wealth stayed home. Even with the constant interruption of education and the almost total lack of opportunity for Palestinians living in the territories, they are undereducated but not backward, just deprived. Arab Americans are an insignificant portion of the Muslim world and less than one-third of the tiny percentage of American Muslims—a nanokernel of the American population as a whole. Nevertheless, in American society, Arabs who are Muslim have become the dominant representation of all Arabs in America through media focus due to terrorist groups and civil chaos in the Middle East.

External forces such as wars, intraethnic and interreligious strife, colonizations, occupations, the fall of the Ottoman Empire, and the creation of the State of Israel all play important roles in how media deployed and continues to deploy representations first offered almost two centuries ago. Internal depictions of Islam and Muslims play a foundational role in how Americans understand the world religion of Islam and the inclinations of its followers.

Newspapers

Many writers report that from 1917 forward, newspapers focused on the conflicts that were occurring in the Middle East/Syria as unembellished news with a few occasional reports on everyday life. Despite the level of chaos nearing the end of Ottoman rule, American reporters chose not to report on the life of the people there.

The descriptions of the conflicts were not uniform in newspapers such as the *New York Times* and magazines such as *Newsweek*. By the time newspaper reporters focused on the Middle East, the theater of World War I had begun, and U.S. troops and their actions took up a great deal of foreign news. Arab Americans kept themselves informed of their old homelands through family communications and their own newspapers. Their money went to families back home and to the war effort, which they joined.

As both a matter of ideological position and a potential contender in the West for dominance, American newspapers told most stories from the point of view of the colonial powers. Arab Americans did not apparently complain about the one-sided coverage.

By 1947, leading newspapers such as the *New York Times* began to mobilize American public support for the creation of the State of Israel as a homeland for Jews, especially those who survived the Nazi holocaust of World War II. The moral mandate to secure a homeland where those atrocities would never happen again pervaded the thoughts of the major powers of the world and especially Jews in America. Israel and its specifically biblical reference for Jews became seen as an ideal location, even though it was in the Middle East. Most Americans were not privy to the political wrangling happening behind the scenes with Britain, which held a mandate over the region. Reports of the horrors of World War II and the killings, massacres, and concentration camps were sent back from the various fronts in Western and Eastern Europe. Even though U.S. government officials would not permit Jews to immigrate to America, they did support a homeland of their own; American Jews lobbied hard for Israel.

Although the final creation of the State of Israel would take over much of Palestinian lands, at this point in history negotiations were still ongoing between two Semitic peoples. The need to survive for both Arabs and Jews on the land has caused wars, skirmishes, and periodic uprisings that continue into the 21st century.

Much of the ensuing conflict from 1956 through 1987 in the Middle East centered on the region previously known as Greater Syria and Palestine as well as Egypt. American newspapers covered the Suez War, the 1967 Six-Day War, and the 1973 Yom Kippur War. Although schools for Palestinians had largely been closed and large numbers of youths were left without education, little of this was reported. Arabs in the region were

Cars line up waiting for gas during the gas crisis of the early 1970s. (National Archives)

spoken of as uncivilized, uninterested in education for their children, and generally cunning derelicts who lived in poor sanitation.

The year 1973 proved to be a year of tumultuous change, as in addition to the Arab-Israeli war and other foreign news, there was an orchestrated gas crisis in the United States. Arab members of the Organization of Petroleum Exporting Countries (OPEC) imposed an embargo against the United States in retaliation for the U.S. decision to resupply the Israeli military in Israel's war against the Palestinians. In the United States citizens lined up, sometimes for hours, for gasoline for their cars. Gas stations ran out of gasoline and diesel fuel, preventing smooth transport of people and goods. A deal had to be struck before the winter heating oil season. One effect was American recognition of its overwhelming dependency on foreign oil. Over the first six months of the embargo, newspapers and television news reported quadrupled gasoline prices.

Today, OPEC controls 42 percent of the world's oil supply, 61 percent of its exports, and 80 percent of proven oil reserves. This state of affairs in 1973 caused a two-year recession and increased inflation in the United States. Foreign affairs were brought to every American's doorstep, and even though it was Arab-originated, there was only moderate castigation of Arabs in the news.

While newspapers reported on foreign affairs (though many times in a biased way), political cartoons remained largely out of the fray regarding Arabs. Though political cartoons focus on injustices of all sorts, aiming to cause society to reflect on itself, Arabs in America and the Middle East mostly escaped the pens of these graphic artists. The major focus was instead on blacks, Chinese, Native Americans, and the Irish, to name a few ethnic and racial groups, in the first half of the 20th century. World War II had turned most Americans' attention to Japanese Americans, with accusations that they were spies and subversives. Almost all were forced into relocation and incarceration camps in the western interior of the country in 1942 after the attack on Pearl Harbor. This forced internment included people with as little as $1/16$ Japanese blood. This horrific situation lasted for three years, with Japanese Americans losing their homes and businesses, which other Americans looted, took over, or burned.

The McCarthy era followed on the heels of the paranoia about the Japanese with its focus on the potential and sometimes real infiltration of the Communist Party into America. The House Un-American Activities Committee had the task of uncovering and identifying for the public anti-American or procommunist activities. As the eyes of the country moved from World War II to the civil rights movement, the fear of Germans and Japanese was transferred to African Americans, Native Americans, and various immigrant groups. They became targets of suspicion and objects of infiltration, undergoing surveillance of the groups and religious organizations they belonged to.

Today there is a push by the government to institute bans against Muslims from seven (and counting) countries from entering the United States and preventing American citizens from traveling to those countries. All of the countries are Arab countries and majority Muslim states. The executive order's rationale—issued on the day of Holocaust Remembrance, when a similar ban was issued against Jews—is to prevent terrorists from entering the United States. The envisioning that began long ago with images painted by words and in caricature continues.

The Visual Background

The correlation between visual images of Arabs in the United States and world events is very pronounced. Much of the foundation of those visual narratives comes from Protestant Christian missionaries' tracts on their perceptions of predominantly Muslim Greater Syria. In the 19th century, letters from missionaries home to relatives in the United States were filled with prose describing the persons met in the Ottoman Empire.

One missionary evoked terror and foreboding in an 1820 letter to his sister, describing one person as "of gigantic stature, long beard, fierce eyes, a turban on his head" (Marr 2006, 82). The fact that many of the men they met had both pistols and a sword lent credence to thoughts of the barbarity of the Muslim world that had already been captured in the prose of European writers' encounters. As American missionaries traveled to the Holy Land in Jerusalem through Arab-held lands, further descriptions such as "a place cursed of God and given over to iniquity" (Marr 2006, 83) depicted the horrors of the Ottoman Empire.

Letters and diary entries and the threat of Islam and its despotism to the young republic of America began shaping American perceptions of the Arab Muslim world. In 1788 the *New Haven Gazette* stated that "the faith of Mahomet [Muhammed], wherever it is established, is unified with despotic power" (Marr 2006, 21). Yet it was the Barbary Wars that made those perceptions more concrete as statesmen such as Benjamin Franklin wrote diary entries on their capture by Muslims. In time, stories reemerged of Captain John Smith's enslavement and release by Muslims. The ending days of the Ottoman Empire contributed to a need to know why this empire failed so thoroughly, and the answer for many of those in power in the United States was its adherence to a vile, un-Christian religion; its violence; and general amoral living and corruption. Though the Arab Middle East was subjugated under the Ottoman Empire, in the first immigration records the Syrians and Lebanese were initially called Turks. Here again, external forces played a large role in defining Arab American identity. The media was also one of those external forces that shaped identity and perceptions of identity that came to be challenged. All of these narratives and the caricatures that accompanied them formed much of the background information for early filmmakers.

Let's Quietly Go to the Movies

During and immediately after World War I, makers of silent movies employed the theme of "us against them" in a widely watched series of intense dramas. Movies such as *Tragedy of the Desert* (1917), *Ali Baba and the Forty Thieves* (1917), *The Sheik* (1921), and *The Thief of Bagdad* (1924) became a singular category of romantic swash-buckling films that provided context for Western understanding of the Middle East for almost 40 years. Actors including Douglas Fairbanks and Theodosia Goodman earned their marquee billing by acting as white heroes saving women from licentious brutal Arab men or as seductive Arab women, respectively.

Ironically, what viewers of these tales saw was a parade of supposed Arabs: Jews, Chinese, and other "exotic" women played the roles of Arab women, and an array of white American men played the roles of both American saviors and villainous Arabs. Rudolph Valentino's role in *The Sheik* is a prime example of this.

Early in Arab American history, "Arab" became conflated with "Muslim" and "Islam." Stereotypes of endlessly sandy landscapes, bejeweled clothing, and poorly kept slaves were used and are still being used to convey information about geography and culture. According to silent movies, Arabs had no cities and instead existed in clusters of huts

A scene from *Son of the Sheik*, 1926. Here, Rudolph Valentino plays to the American stereotype. (Archive Photos/Getty Images)

(one did not see in the distance more than a hint of a town) surrounded by sand. Palaces, on the other hand, were clearly situated somewhere other than the sand, but astute views find that there is no definite geography. Even when Arab or white women are rescued, the desolate environment again appears miraculously until they reach the encampment of the "saviors."

Civic institutions are rarely portrayed; there are no police beyond tribal councils, no hospitals, and only a few marketplaces. Much of the action takes place near watering holes for people and camels, inside palaces, or actually in transit on camels. Barracks for Western armies exist in some movies, but the implication is that they are outside of towns and are barricaded against the barbarity. The scenery is dark, ominous, mysterious, and delightfully thrilling in its exotic juxtaposition of light and dark. Women's spaces inside palaces are light and fun-filled but guarded boudoirs with curtained large bathing pools. Wives are seen scheming against each other for first place in the mind of the husband. Their veils are transparent and are constantly in the process of being removed by the women themselves, their lovers, or strange men.

Arab women were variously portrayed by any actress who looked exotic and foreign, giving birth to the term "vamp," according to Professor Tania Kamal-Eldin. Arab women did not live in families or with a family. Rather, they were seen as living in harems of many women, all married to one old man. In the world of Arab women, loyalty was to the husband only, not to any of the other women. Slave women were loyal to their mistresses, who were seen as treating them dismissively. Belly dancing became the symbol of the sexual availability of women. Through these movies, viewers were transported to a mysterious world filled with luxury, beautiful women who needed to be saved, and poor slave women often locked in the destiny of their owners. Owners of this luxury are amoral, vile men who follow a religion that commands them to wipe at the sand while praying, marry many women, cheat, steal, and lie. Nevertheless, all of these elements make for intrigue and both unrequited and true love.

This idea of the exotic and mysterious was widely promoted in 19th-century romantic literature and became a staple of early film. These women were seductive, cunning, enchanting, and scantily dressed with see-through veils, which could always be easily removed. They were also often pictured in large baths with teams of slave women and eunuchs to wait on them and keep men out, which was rarely accomplished (thus creating drama).

Edward Lane's translation of the *Arabian Nights* (1839–1841) added to the background information of the lands of the Arabs. Though centered on flying horses, magic lamps, jinns, and other fantasies, Lane thought that his translation depicted Middle Eastern life. His endnotes did not endure in many publications, but his illustrations of fantasy did and would later provide the fodder for cartoon re-creations. From *Arabian Nights* emerged a series of characters such as Scheherazade, Alladin, Ali Baba, Sinbad the Sailor, and Ja'far. This book and others came to America in the luggage of travelers and statesmen and was republished, and from there the images traveled to the cinema. As early screenwriters sought stories, *Arabian Nights* became an endless source of characters, characterizations, and descriptions of scenery.

Posters advertising these films used pencil sketches of the book illustrations, taking artistic license to increase the interest of moviegoers to not only go to the cinema but also absorb these swash-buckling tales of intrigue and romance during the time of economic recovery from the

Great Depression. The large repertoire of images from *Arabian Nights* has lasted almost a century. Some of these silent films have been remastered in recent decades due to their popularity.

I Can Now Hear at the Movies

The first American talkie was *The Jazz Singer* (1927). With synchronized sound and full feature-length timing, the film heralded the end of silent movies as a new spectacular form of entertainment took over. In the movie Jackie Rabinowitz, son of Jewish immigrants, leaves home to avoid taking his father's place as a cantor. Jackie strives to take his voice and talents to the movie screen, where he appears in blackface, which becomes his identifier. This movie ushered in the talkie to entertainment-hungry American moviegoers.

Eddie Cantor, also known for performing in blackface, played the leading role in *Ali Baba Goes to Town* (1937), a comedy about an American hobo who goes to Hollywood, falls asleep on the set of *Arabian Nights,* and dreams that he is in Baghdad, introducing Franklin Roosevelt's New Deal to the sultan. The old silent movie *The Thief of Bagdad* was reintroduced in 1940. Baghdad is portrayed as a place of violence with the similarly archetypal stereotypes of sand, genies, magic carpets, sultans, and beautiful scantily clad women. *Arabian Nights,* the foundational literary text, was made into a movie in 1942. It was a lavish spectacle put on during the war years, with a Dominican-born actress playing Scheherazade. Movie reviewers saw this movie as a much-needed deflection from the anxieties resulting from the death and social upheaval caused by the war, much like the necessity of social acceptance of Roosevelt's New Deal was explained to the average American in *Ali Baba Goes to Town.*

Bagdad, released in 1949, starred redheaded actress Maureen O'Hara as a Bedouin princess (even though there are few if any redheaded Arab women). In this story, a backward Arab princess is educated after becoming civilized in England, only to find her father murdered by one of the Arab tribes. The romance comes in the attempts at courtship by the pasha who is hosting her, while intrigue is found in her search for justice. Another all-American cast portrays Arabs in *Kismet* as a ruler goes undercover to get to know his subjects.

Images that were cemented on the American psyche about the nature of Arab Americans had a connection with global politics. In *Arabs in American Cinema 1894–1930* (2013), Abdelmajid Hajji provides a thorough examination of the problems with portrayals and the connections with global politics. Arabs represent the evil "other" that is in opposition to the law, order, and progress of the West. Superstition overrides reason; the Middle East has fallen into decay, death, and backwardness in the face of the youth, vigor, and innovation of the West.

This analysis further confirms that Arab immigrant experiences were different. Arab immigrants were not only seeking to settle but also creating new identities for themselves while different new identities were being created for them. On the one hand, the new identity was created by the new circumstances. On the other hand, fanciful identities had already been created for them to either accept or reject. For most, survival took priority. The Barbary Wars and Protestant missionary incursions formed a platform on which all that was Arab would be placed.

Once Europe placed itself as the West and the Arab world as the Middle East between Europe and the Far East, the die was cast. The West became the home of civility, while the Middle East was a place of mystery, intrigue, violence, and sin. In this world, no civilized man or woman was safe from the licentiousness that reigned amid outrageous wealth and pure corruption. Theatrical exaggerations of flying carpets, genies in lanterns, and caricatures of malevolence served as entertainment that could be enjoyed by all. This was the Middle East—static and unchanging. The men were thieves and rogues, while the women only pretended piety behind veils as they schemed to become favored wives. Arabs were prime candidates for saving and civilizing. They had no rules of conduct, no policing, and no redeeming religious or other values beyond their inherent lust, avarice, and larceny.

Images from movies became a part of American cultural knowledge, cemented with the newness and excitement of cinema. Cinema itself spoke to the creativity of America and its development of new devices. Cinema also rearranged social life, as it allowed Americans in created spaces of small audiences of strangers to be both entertained and informed by new media. This format was not available initially anywhere else in the world. Families who had available free time and money could now add going to the movies to their recreational time. Of course, blacks and Indians were not welcomed for decades; when they were allowed, they were seated in balconies. The stories of these movies and their contents became conversations in many places, and an image of Arab Americans began its trek through generations.

By World War II, Arab lives in the Middle East again became fodder for movies that served to entertain in a time of uncertainty. Clearly the Middle East was being reshaped again during the height of colonialism. The reasons why this land needed attention were clear: it needed saving and order.

Movies in the Home: The TV

The first successful demonstration of electronic television, designed by a 21-year-old inventor named Philo Taylor Farnsworth, occurred in 1927. By 1939, RCA was able to televise the New York World's Fair including a speech by President Franklin D. Roosevelt, who was the first president to ever appear on television. Newscasts began in 1941. By 1949, Americans who lived within range of the growing number of television stations could watch *The Texaco Star Theater* (1948) with Milton Berle and the children's program *Howdy Doody*. The social function of smoking was also introduced, because the tobacco industry was a major sponsor that demanded that its adult stars keep cigarettes in their mouths. For families who could afford television sets, the television became a babysitter for after school until dinnertime. Sometimes neighbors gathered socially at the homes that had a television, much like they did for radio broadcasts. The 1950s were a time for inventions that dramatically changed the lives of middle- and upper-class American women: stoves with griddles on top, ironing machines, automatic toasters, and even McDonald's. These inventions significantly reduced housework time and left time for family entertainment.

The magical character of television brought with it the opportunity of cartoons, and Arab caricatures were not ignored in this medium. Cartoon versions of the *Arabian Nights* were presented during children's viewing hours, affecting what children learned of the Arab world.

As scholar Jack Shaheen (1984) asserts and as confirmed by child psychologists, television has its strongest impact on children. While other American children were learning about an exotic world, Arab American children were seeing exaggerated pictures of their parent's homelands. Obviously this had a profound effect on their developing minds, as they asked questions about the flying carpets, genies, and large bathtubs of people that they thought their parents knew about. Cartoons further depended on images from the *Arabian Nights* in *Wonder Woman, Woody Woodpecker, Popeye,* and even *Porky Pig.*

Melodrama has always been a highlight of television, and adult audiences have been attracted to it in all of its forms. Its best form, however, is the detective or police story. With the components of chase, escape, arrest, trial, heroic sacrifice, and a last-minute rescue, every successful melodrama holds the attention of its viewers. Here the images of Islam become background as private detectives such as Simon and Simon, Jim Rockford, Jonathan and Jennifer Hart, and Frank Cannon find themselves pursuing criminals. Many of these detective stories have been reengineered digitally for 21st-century viewers. Sheehan asserts that in particular Frank

Cannon is seen outwitting dim-witted Arabs, although he occasionally helps innocent Arabs outwit the police. Arabs are still depicted as deceptive, untrustworthy, larcenous, and murderous, as if it is a genetic trait.

An episode of *The Rockford Files* (1974–1980) titled "Three Day Affair with a Thirty Day Escrow" begins with some Arab roughnecks dragging Rockford out of bed. Of course, Rockford defeats them all and escapes. Intrigue and romance quickly follow as Rockford finds out that they were really after his friend, who is entangled with a married Arab woman. This harkens back to the claim that the modesty of Arab women is a ruse, as they are sexually unrestrained even when married and thus must be contained and closely watched by fathers, brothers, and husbands. Though Jim Rockford saves the situation and the woman's life (from execution for adultery), viewers are reminded that white men not only save white women who have fallen into Arab hands but also save Arab women from barbaric customs.

By the advent of 24-hour news in the 1980s, murderous acts previously conducted by swords or discreetly carried knives had been replaced by beheadings; murderers became terrorists. The Iranian hostage crisis was broadcast with student's threats to kill American embassy workers. Viewers of this programming were greeted with throngs of chador-clad Iranian Muslim women in the streets of Tehran calling for the demise of America. The shah of Iran's intimate ties to the American government and subsequent dismissal of all but the elite of Iran was not reported until much later.

The parallels in types of violence between drama and news were too obvious to ignore. William Conrad's *Cannon* character tracks down Arab terrorists who are doing the usual kidnapping with threats of murder. Shaheen notes one particular episode of *Return of the Saint* where there are Palestinian assassins and Israeli agents. The intrigue of the ongoing strife of Arab-Israeli affairs was brought to American homes in a fictionalized account. Iranians have become Arab along with Palestinians.

Television constructs and then circulates many Americans' opinions of foreign affairs. The conflicts "over there" are brought to the United States and filtered through the thoughts of producers and directors. Entertainment is made political. As focus was once again on the Arab world, attention was especially drawn to the disparities in the living of the wealthy and the poor, the lack of civil institutions, and the plight of women. This situation is only lightened in comedic programming. Comedy is supposed to bring entertainment and joy to issues that are otherwise sometimes sensitive, but to many Arab Americans it brought more caricature and embarrassment along with the humor.

According to Jack Shaheen, "The comedy of the Seventies and Eighties might well be dubbed the era of the Arab joke" (1984, 55). In a famous Arab scam run by the Federal Bureau of Investigation (FBI) in 1980, agents apparently posed as Arab oil barons in an attempt to ferret out corrupt politicians on Capitol Hill. This operation, dubbed ABSCAM, is asserted to be the beginning of a host of jokes involving Arabs. The agents' phony Arabic names became everyday monikers for corruption, scheming, and deceitfulness. Americans were unceremoniously duped, as the names were not Arabic names, and although the barons claimed to be from Lebanon, there are no oil wells there. Here "otherness" and the lack of tools to know how one is being deceived is on display.

In his 1980 Thanksgiving Day special, Alan King used the closed-circuit films of the FBI to introduce a skit involving an interrogation of members of Congress that shows the duplicity of Arabs and the dumbness of the congressmen. Walter Cronkite confusedly cast the affair as "alleged bribery by Arab interests." In what was supposed to be satire, King followed his initial skit with comedian Danny Thomas (Arab Christian) as the "King of Lebanon," asserting that "Syria is keeping the peace in Lebanon," and "they are doing a good job—Lebanon is in pieces" (Shaheen 1984, 56–57). While many Americans found this hilarious, given the elaborate turbans worn and the personality of these comedians, Arab Americans had mixed reactions to the humorous slant given to a very serious situation. However, most Americans were unaware of where Lebanon was or what was really going on there.

In an episode of *The Sonny and Cher Comedy Hour*, all-American singers sang "This Land Is Your Land," smiling as they sat on top of a map of the United States. Suddenly, a group of Arabs snuck out from behind the curtains to steal portions of the map. The political side of this seemingly innocent and uplifting episode was marred by the ongoing oil crisis; hatred of Arabs was mounting as Americans formed long lines waiting for shrinking gasoline availability.

Film, Fiction, and TV after 9/11

After the horrific events of September 11, 2001, Americans were terrified. Their enemies were supposed to be over there, not here. Politicians, newscasters, filmmakers, and writers all turned the terror and fear into opportunities for commodities—getting elected to public office, getting more TV time, and obtaining funding for more films or fodder for more mystery thrillers. Fear drove Americans to watch more TV, go to the movies more often, and buy mystery thrillers. Newscasters and politicians confirmed the dangers in the movies, on TV, and in the paperbacks they read. The dangers in the mystery thriller novels had to be real, because newscasters talked about them on the evening news.

There was a significant increase in the number of movies involving Arabs and anyone else who could be envisioned as Arab. The first such TV series of the post–9/11 era, *24*, aired on November 6, 2001. Each episode was to cover 24 hours in Jack Bauer's life as a counterterrorism expert. The novelty of this series produced by the Fox network was that the narration was in real time. Over 192 episodes, Bauer's task was to thwart terrorist plots. The real-time narration of each episode kept viewers riveted to their television sets. Arabs were either terrorists, sly informants who could not be trusted, or on rare occasion allies.

The use of special effects such as split screen and jump cuts were deployed as a form of storytelling to assist the audience in keeping up with the intense twists and turns of the program. The action was relentless, and the evident stress of the central characters was front stage. Many stories were told in one story inside of the 24 hours, and the techniques used enabled viewers to feel as if they were there. This TV series was addictive. It also instilled more fear of Arabs.

Clearly *24* shaped what was to come on television and influenced what was to appear in the movies. Executives in Hollywood and scriptwriters for television both were trying to figure out how to exploit the theme of terrorism and at the same time avoid the risk associated with overkill. Hollywood removed many images of the World Trade Center from their movies to avoid offending or upsetting people in the immediate years after the events of that day. Scriptwriters for programs set in New York, such as *Law & Order,* showed no scenes with the World Trade Center, though they were occasionally referenced.

Scholars identify three stages to classify the era of media regard for the political and social climate after 9/11. First were movies that did not talk about 9/11, mention it, or even imply that it had happened, especially when the story was set in New York. Then as fear subsided, writers and directors used incrementally larger references to 9/11 and even included some plots related to terrorism. In the last stage, movies and TV shows dealt exclusively with terrorism.

The television series *Homeland* first aired in 2011 and followed a successful line of programming regarding psychological thrillers. This series focuses on the people meant to protect America and their continuing personal problems. The central protagonist, a Central Intelligence Agency (CIA) agent, is a closet bipolar personality who has fixated on a rescued agent she thinks is a terrorist threat to the United States. In this action-packed thriller, audiences are toggled between the personal mental problems of one CIA agent and the attempts to make the suspected agent a double agent. Arabs provide the background mostly as terrorists, reinforcing existing stereotypes.

NCIS, another acclaimed TV series, is a lighter, softer version of *24.* Legal procedural shows all had episodes dealing with terrorism. Several shows, such as *The Practice, Family Law,* and *Judging Amy,* had episodes in which an Arab or Persian character is picked up by Homeland Security or the FBI, and the lawyers are stymied by "classified information" in trying to understand what their client did, what the client's motives were, and how to defend the client. Fears of the erosion of civil liberties proliferated in the early days of the war on terror.

The armed forces of the United States and other security agencies all find themselves marketed as the major strong arms against terrorism. The *Transformers* film series is a perfect example both of the stages of media regard and of marketing. In the first film there is no mention of the war on terror, even though the army base where much of the action happens is in Qatar. No one mentions the possibility of a terrorist attack, though the culprits are assumed to be from Iran, North Korea, or China. In the second film, the special forces are hunting the Decepticons all over the world. By the third film, however, the Decepticons have become terrorists who execute a 9/11-type event on a citywide scale in Chicago. Filmmakers evoke imagery of 9/11 throughout the entire scene by knocking over buildings, setting them on fire, and showing people jumping from them. The question of what happens if Americans make concessions to terrorists is answered in this film.

Adam Sandler finds a new persona for himself in *Reign over Me* and *You Don't Mess with the Zohan.* In the first movie, he is a 9/11 widower who is helped by his friend (played by Don Cheadle) to overcome his grief. In the second movie, the issues of terrorism are directly dealt with through the frame of the Arab-Israeli conflict. Sandler is a counterterror operative in the movie *Iron Man,* where the superhero finds his beginning in Afghanistan. Even though the culprits aren't Islamist terrorists, the fact that they are not is not made apparent. For all intents and purposes, Arab terrorists are holding Tony Stark.

Most unnerving and simultaneously riveting is the film *Unthinkable.* Samuel L. Jackson plays the role of the ultimate interrogator of terrorists. The film focuses on the psychological toll that extreme interrogation techniques have on practitioners and subjects. Viewers are left with the question of whether or not the interrogators can be as bad as the terrorists themselves. In this film, a convert to Islam releases a tape showing him in three nondescript storage rooms, each of which may contain a nuclear bomb. Jackson is the CIA consultant who is sent to interrogate the suspect, who has remarkably allowed himself to be caught. Several subjects are addressed in this film, including the use of torture to extract information to save lives versus the inhumane nature of torture. Other actors in the film question the length to which the United States should go to extract information. This film is horrifying (as it was meant to be), as the nation is seen as struggling with the demons of terrorism.

This movie is juxtaposed in many ways to *The House of Sand and Fog,* which is a tale of immigrant loss and resettlement in the United States and the story of a young female alcoholic who is recovering her life. We see the immigrant family as one who had wealth and position in Iran, but everything was lost with the change in government, so they moved to the United States. They believe that they have to live as if they are still in Iran, meaning that the home and its accessories have to reveal wealth; otherwise, they will be unable to marry off their daughter to an appropriate suitor. The immigrant man was once an officer of high status who has now been reduced to working in highway construction in America. He leaves home as if he is going to an office job, changing clothing in a hotel washroom, and reverses this procedure at the end of the day so that his family is unaware of how he keeps food on the table.

For some immigrants in similar situations, fleeing new regimes and their countries and becoming exiles is a change in status, lifestyle, and family relationships. For many, the old wealth is never reassembled, nor is the grandeur of the old lifestyle. In this movie, a remnant of the old environment is captured in a particular house that was formally owned by the alcoholic woman who never opened her mail and thus lost the house to taxes. What ensues is a conflict of values, integrity, and wills. The immigrant man was stereotyped as an Arab man even though he was of Iranian descent. Amid the environment of the United States, Iranians (and even sometimes South Asians) become Arab.

Issues of homeland security became paramount; security was focused on preventing Arab groups from committing acts of terror. The civil liberties of American citizens were pitted against the need to secure the nation. The lists of Arab terror groups grew exponentially, and complicated terminology followed. By the mid-20th century, there were Islamic radicals, jihadists, radical jihadists, radical extremists, and so on. What they all had in common supposedly was Islam, Arabness (predominantly), and a willingness to commit suicide to attack American and European targets. Arab American community members were all categorized as terrorists—actual, potential, or supporters.

Arab American responses to these changes have also occurred in stages. The events of 9/11 completely stunned the Arab community, especially since the attackers were Arabs. The immediate reaction of non–Arab Americans was also shock. Some in the non–Arab American community instantly reached out to Arab communities to ask what they could do to help protect them against backlash. These instances of outreach to a once relatively invisible community were welcomed and spurred the Arab community to begin understanding itself as a part of the fabric of the larger society.

Many in the Arab community were recent (less than 20 years) immigrants and their children, who were still challenged by the rapid changes in the social fabric of the United States. The problems of settling into an identity rose again after 9/11. Many Arabs had settled into ethnic enclaves in metropolitan areas across the nation. Since many were small entrepreneurs, their businesses (including groceries, clothing stores, and other services) could be found in their areas of cities. In these areas both the signage on stores and the major language was Arabic. After 9/11, there was a need to demonstrate belonging to the fabric of American life and an abhorrence of the tragic events of 9/11. Many Arabs were confused at how quickly hatred of their ethnicity had spread. What they didn't realize was the impact of the movies, TV programming, and mystery thriller books on children growing up in America post–9/11. Many of these children, now teenagers and young adults, have only one picture of Arab Americans: terrorists. Newer documents have sought to mediate these depictions by showing Arab Americans in everyday life as business people, students, and professionals, but change is slow.

Many Americans are avid readers of romance novels, mystery thrillers, self-help books, and religious books. Ideas about other cultures are often gleaned from these texts. On the shelves in the stores after 9/11 there were many anti-Islam and anti-Muslim books. They were bought and read both as authoritative viewpoints and guides for understanding what was going on.

Texts such as *Extreme Islam: Anti-American Propaganda of Muslim Fundamentalism, Islam Unveiled: The Antichrist Revealed,* and *Because They Hate* created a new category on Amazon. These texts were not available in Arab neighborhoods, around Muslim places of worship, or in university bookstores. The stereotyping and hatred endorsed in the pages of these books shaped some of the violence against Arabs and Muslims in the country. Mystery thrillers began to have Arab terrorists as planners in complicated schemes to attack U.S. airports, bus stations, and business districts.

Americans in various faith communities have had many responses to the issues of terrorism, civil liberties, and Islam as one faith tradition. All Americans agree that the specter of terrorist acts is something no one wants to contemplate, but the banning or extreme vetting of one ethnicity from the country is up for contentious debate. Many Arab countries are excluded from Trump's ban. Does this mean that particular national groups are okay and are being identified away from their ethnic heritage? Can one country do that to another country for any reason? What happens to pride in one's national heritage and ethnicity? For Arab Americans, the answers are clear. They are Arab Americans who are proud of their heritage, which is older than that of the United States, and they are proud of their various religious heritages.

Given the ethnic diversity within the larger category of Arab, communication of the news and the threats is complicated. Early immigrants to the United States began to publish newspapers to communicate with each other across the country and with family back home. Post–9/11 newspapers were needed to communicate the welfare of communities inside the United States as a priority to information about the news from the ancestral home. Current Arab American news media is relatively young. Newspapers remain the staple of the community, while news websites are currently the most prominent sector—though much of it still focuses on community news and events.

According to a study done by the Pew Research Center in 2012, a number of papers are witnessing rising circulation (Brown, Guskin, and Mitchell 2012). Some new publications have been launched, though all are struggling to recover financially from the economic recession of 2007 and the competition of digital technology and social media. Radio programming aimed at Arab Americans is declining in the face of limited advertising revenue, as is much other radio programming. Arab American television remains almost nonexistent, as does Arab American TV or radio news. Since the United States withdrew its broadcasting space for Al Jazeera English in 2016, no competitors have filled the space. The *New York Times* analysis of this particular situation was that it was "a lesson in both the limitations of public diplomacy and the obstacles to providing high quality television journalism" (Ibish 2016).

The absence of media programming directed at the community has encouraged engagement of other media. However, the absence of media has further put identity in question. In the 2011 American community survey, the U.S. Census Bureau reported that there were close to 1.8 million Arab Americans living in the United States, an increase of about 47 percent in population size from 2000. The sheer size of the community, however, brings into question even more concerns with identity.

Interestingly, Arabs began to tell stories of their homelands, which consisted mostly of the tragedies of the abuse of women, the abuses of children, and corruption. These stories set out to preserve a distinct cultural heritage and demonstrate the complexity of Arab American experiences while unwittingly feeding back into the stereotypes that formed the Arab identity in America in the early 20th century. The stereotypes in the 1990s, especially with movies such as *True Lies*, focused on Arab and Arab American culture as synonymous with religious fundamentalism, without any background of cultural heritage and pride in the cultural and artistic history. It is a story of a terrorist who was smuggling weapons of mass destruction to the United States hidden inside of Egyptian artifacts. The Arab is willing to sacrifice precious Egyptian artifacts for nefarious ends. In this tale, corruption is not at issue when the potential of American destruction is a possibility.

In novels such as Khaled Hosseini's *The Kite Runner*, Afghans are transported into the world of the Arab. The Afghans pictured are upper middle class or upper class with a secular outlook, but they are Arabs to viewers. Because the author is an Afghan, there is an assumption of truth in the story that is being viewed. Afghanistan's turmoil of confusion, briberies, and desperate people reminds moviegoers of the other tales of the Middle East. One major feature of this story is a tale of friendship that survives distance. The heartrending tale of one friend settling into America while the other deals with sexual abuse in the life of his son is reminiscent of the pictures painted about the Middle East.

The Reluctant Fundamentalist makes the personal political and vice versa. How does a young Pakistani man who by his own intellect has made his way from Pakistan to the United States on a scholarship to attend one of the most elite U.S. universities turn to fundamentalism? As with *The Kite Runner*, this book was also made into a movie. The main character, Changez (implying change for English viewers), is living the American Dream. He is a star employee at an elite valuation firm that works all over the world and is dating a young woman from upper-class society. The events of 9/11 change him profoundly. His identity is in seismic shift as he finds himself under suspicion everywhere until he comes to terms with his markings inside his cultural heritage.

Changez's story presents readers and viewers with one inside testimony of how the American Dream can become a nightmare. Changez is reluctantly drawn into the fray of politics and a born identity that he was abandoning. This book is about a Pakistani man, and much of the scenery is in Pakistan, but for American viewers he is Arab, and Arabs flew planes into the World Trade Center and the Pentagon. The events of 9/11 changed many non–Middle Easterners into Arabs.

A small genre of literature written by Arab Christians made its way into the American mainstream. This literature revealed an unabiding hatred of Islam and Muslims and presented a warning to American society to be wary of permitting the presence of Muslims on American soil. Their texts were mailed to various University professors throughout the country for review. These texts were stringent in their assault on the religion of Islam and the prior and current actions of both Islamic governments on Christian citizens and terrorist attacks. These texts, written under pseudonyms, were expanded by the contributions of women.

Profiles

Khaled Hosseini (1952–), an Afghan American novelist and physician, was born in Kabul, Afghanistan. His family of diplomats sought asylum in the United States after a military coup when he was 15 years old. As the son of diplomats, his upbringing was quite cosmopolitan, as the family lived in Iran and Paris before coming to the United States. Hosseini's three novels about Afghanistan and its people's loves and tragedies all remained on the *New York Times* best-seller lists for months.

Tania Kamal-Eldin (n.d.–) is an independent filmmaker and educator, especially on women and Middle Eastern issues. She examines the interactions of gender, race, and cross-cultural representation. Two of her films are used widely in women and gender studies: *Covered: The Hejab in Cairo, Egypt* and *Hollywood Harems*.

Jack Shaheen (1935–2017) was a writer and a lecturer specializing in the issues around racial and ethnic stereotypes, especially focusing on Arab Americans. He was born in Pittsburgh to Christian Lebanese Arab immigrants. Shaheen's text *Reel Bad Arabs: How Hollywood Vilifies a People* provided groundbreaking scholarship for students of cultural studies, journalism, and communication. As a journalism professor at Southern Illinois University, his critical work set a standard for stereotyping in movies.

References

Brown, Heather, Emily Guskin, and Amy Mitchell. "Arab-American Media: Bringing News to a Diverse Community." Pew Research Center, November 28, 2012, http://www.journalism.org/2012/11/28/arabamerican-media/.

Hajji, Abdelmajid. *Arabs in American Cinema (1894–1930): Flappers Meet Sheiks in New Movie Genre.* n.d.: CreateSpace Independent Publishing Platform, 2013.

Hosseini, Khaled. *The Kite Runner.* New York: Riverhead Books, 2013.

Ibish, Hussein. "Why America Turned Off Al Jazeera." *New York Times,* February 17, 2016, https://www.nytimes.com/2016/02/18/opinion/why-america -turned-off-al-jazeera.html.

Kamal-Eldin, Tania. *Hollywood Harems.* Women Make Movies, 1999. Videocassette (25 min.).

Marr, Timothy. *The Cultural Roots of American Islamicism.* Cambridge: Cambridge University Press, 2006.

Said-Moorhouse, Lauren, and Ryan Browne. "Donald Trump Wants 'Extreme Vetting' of Immigrants. What Is the US Doing Now?" CNN, August 16, 2016, http://www.cnn.com/2016/08/16/politics/how-us-vets-immigrants -donald-trump-extreme-vetting/index.html.

Shaheen, Jack. *The TV Arab.* Bowling Green, OH: Bowling Green State University Popular Press, 1984.

CHAPTER EIGHT

The 9/11 Generations

Children just beginning kindergarten, Arab adolescents, and young adults returning from summers in the Middle East all experienced trauma due to the events of 9/11. The psychological trauma of childhood and adolescence has long perplexed mental and physical health practitioners, primarily because the patient rarely has the vocabulary or confidence to speak.

Child health, like adult health, includes behavioral, mental, and physical health. When these large areas are taken into account with social constructions such as racism and/or discrimination, the actual breadth and depth of concerns is life-threatening. Health professionals have a clear definition of racism that is important to recapture here.

According to Human Rights Watch,

> Racism is present when there is any distinction, exclusion, restriction, or preference made based on race, color, descent, or nation/ethnic origin which has the purpose or effect of nullifying or impairing the recognition, enjoyment, or exercise, on an equal footing of human rights and fundamental freedoms in the political, economic, social, cultural, or any other field of public life. ("World Report 2001")

Researchers have found that self-reported experiences and expectations of discrimination were associated with depressive symptoms such as low self-esteem/self-worth and anxiety in preadolescents and adolescents. Many of these symptoms were directly caused by school stress and resulted in conduct disorders. Parental racial discrimination was directly tracked to child distress (general anxiety and depression), independent of the child's own experiences. The inability of the parent to recover often

The World Trade Center in the aftermath of September 11, 2001. (U.S. Department of Defense)

resulted in withdrawn behaviors, somatic complaints, anxiety, and depression in the child.

Importantly, during young adulthood and adolescence, many minority youths start to make meaning of their ethnic and racial group membership as a core aspect of their identity. They become increasingly aware of any negative societal views of and prejudices toward their group. Those groups (such as Arab Americans) have experienced undue negative views, outright racism, and discrimination toward their community especially since 9/11. At a time when normative processes of human development regarding identity development take place, many Arab youths are vulnerable, though this is also a time when these very same processes can provide protective cover.

The longer immigrants reside in the United States, the more likely they are to have exposure to bias and discrimination, although these issues can be particularly important for immigrants in the context of anti-immigration legal policies and the social messaging around them. Persistent exposure to incidents of racism always affect physical health by creating demands on individuals' psychological systems, including those that summon humans to fight or flee. Human systems cannot withstand these heightened states of alertness for long without psychic trauma to one degree or another.

Acts of racism or discrimination toward children or adults because of their immigrant status, legal status, skin tone, or language can and often do contribute to what is called "acculturation stress." Children and adolescents of immigrants have many cultural interactions with members of the dominant culture. They are faced with decisions that require negation of their at-home culture and internalization of dominant culture mores. This in itself induces stress. Arab children are being indoctrinated with Arabness at home yet are chided for that ethnic distinctiveness at school, usually beginning with a mispronunciation of their names. Preadolescents and adolescents are always trying to determine the degree to which they should assimilate (although they call it getting along) and try to get out from under the pressure.

Depending on the degree of stress, many youths will attempt to abandon their support network in the home culture. They tend to fare less well than those who opt to maintain the home culture. The dominant culture is not willing to let the victims of its bullying into the core group, and efforts to force oneself in often wind up with tragic consequences, leaving individuals with no place to go.

Arab and Other American 9/11 Generations

As America was under attack on September 11, 2001, children were sent home from school. It would take a few days to find clear, undamaged passport photos of the perpetrators, and all were Arab. The stigmas mentioned in earlier chapters multiplied thousandsfold. What the *New York Times* called "a spasm of hatred uncoiling in small towns and big cities across the nation—and in rising numbers" (Burch 2017) reached into families, touching even small children of all ethnicities.

American students in elementary, junior high, and high schools across America found their families glued to television sets watching the planes crashing into multiple sites in New York; Somerset County, Pennsylvania; and Virginia. They watched people falling and jumping from buildings. Scores of people, covered in debris, screaming from fear and cuts ran across the streets in loops of film for days. First responders were overwhelmed, as were citizen aides. Makeshift memorials and billboards with pictures of loved ones who were missing immediately were visible everywhere. Children looked to shocked and terrified parents and teachers to explain.

Americans were told that the horrific events in Pennsylvania (with 44 dead), Virginia (with 184 dead), and New York City (with 2,768 dead) were part of a plot carried out by members of a terrorist organization called Al Qaeda. Even many newsreaders could not pronounce the name of the group or the names of its members. Americans in general could say "Arab." Taking cues from adults, most young people became wary of Arab classmates and their families. Two or more young Arab men gathered for any reason were cause for suspicion. Young Arab boys playing soccer raised eyebrows.

Given that adolescence is one defining stage in growth and development, the undifferentiated information absorbed in childhood begins to come into focus. A parent's passing comments about immigrants ruining the country or that they should be deported translated into acts of bullying. Arab kids' funny names, which were often shortened for ease of pronunciation, became indicators that they were related to Osama bin Laden. Arab kids named Osama faced an incredible dilemma. In a signal moment, children attempted to return to the ways of the first Arab immigrants to the United States, changing or modifying names. Sudden unwanted sinister visibility drove almost all to seek invisibility. Those who had thought that they belonged found themselves on the outside of activities in staff meetings, on faculties, and in other workplaces. Those Americans who were the perpetrators of this exclusion were acting in protective mode. They sought to protect America against a clear if undefined enemy.

Pollsters were on the move collecting data about general American attitudes against Arabs, Islam, Al Qaeda, and Muslims, often lumping them into one series of questions. These investigators did not take into account the fact that most Americans think that the followers of Islam are Islamics and that "Muslim" refers to Arab. Since almost all of the polls failed to educate on terminology and were conducted in urban spaces of large cities, much of the attitudes of small-town America were missed and allowed to grow negatively without mediation or clarification. They also did not conduct polls specifically of teachers and students, despite schools being the site of immense bullying.

Most Arab American parents send their children to public schools, and thus there are Arab children from over 20 countries in schools across the nation. While in an extremely diverse country every ethnicity or culture cannot be taught in social science courses, when a particular ethnicity is dominant because of locale, some highlights about their culture have been taught. After 9/11, however, no one wanted to hear about fairness or the woes of Arab and Muslim children. Teachers and administrators in many schools were themselves fearful of Arabs and Muslims and conveyed these attitudes in the classrooms.

Neither the Arab community nor the Muslim community had internal resources to deal with the onslaught of hate mail, phone calls, and negative media coverage that ensued after 9/11. Strategies had not been built to protect the community, even in light of the 1990s and escalating problems glimpsed in the rhetoric of Al Qaeda. Arab leaders were as shocked as other Americans by the horrors and the aftermath. Neighbors and friends alike thought that perhaps they did not know Arabs as well as they thought and vice versa. Communities had to change their ways of being but did so grudgingly and slowly.

One young child, age eight, was the victim of rock throwing as he left school in a small town in Texas. Later that evening he died in the hospital, leaving his family forever devastated. Shockingly, this incident was not reported in the newspapers, the children who committed murder were never disciplined, the adults who encouraged them were never reprimanded, and the school was never involved, as no psychiatric support for his classmates was deemed necessary. Community members found out from a video where the mother recounted the incident.

As researchers, pundits, scholars, and journalists focused on the harm done to adults, the children were left without advocates. The first research done with Arab and Muslim children was published in 2008 by two non-Arab and non-Muslim researchers. Using surveys, focus groups, and in-depth interviews, the articulations of the youths regarding their treatment at home and in the public space is startling.

From 1890 to 1920, the term "hyphenated American" was used in the United States to describe and disparage Americans who were of foreign birth or origin and who displayed an allegiance to a foreign country. It was understood that those who were born in the United States or became naturalized would become American and the "hyphen" would then go away. Today the hyphen, often replaced by a word space, is used to differentiate ethnic and national groups. "Arab American" is one such term used to generalize ethnicity, since there are 22 Arab countries with Arabic language as the common feature. Many young people have been taught to identify as Arab even though they do not speak the language.

One Beginning

Often omitted from conversations about Arab Americans is the psychic trauma of loss of land and homes between 1965 and 1990, causing immigration to the United States. Much of the angst centered on Arab-Israeli issues. In 1968 Sirhan Sirhan, a mentally ill young Palestinian living in Los Angeles, assassinated presidential candidate Robert F. Kennedy. This event caused a heightening of American distrust of claims of Palestinian sovereignty and the ongoing organizing efforts in the United States.

Arabs, and in particular those who were Muslim, were yet again associated with terrorism and extremism.

In 1972, the murders of Israeli Olympians in Munich by a faction of the Palestine Liberation Organization further cemented fears, but those fears were not widely disseminated. Even though the incident happened overseas, surveillance and harassment of Arab Americans by U.S. government agencies increased significantly but was not widely broadcast.

On September 11, 2001, 19 Arab men (predominantly from Saudi Arabia and the United Arab Emirates) boarded planes aimed at causing mass destruction in the eastern United States; the hijacked planes crashed in rural Pennsylvania; Arlington, Virginia; and New York City. All of these attempts were successful to varying degrees. Subsequently, the war on terrorism began against a country, nonstate actors, and Arabs living in the United States.

Constitutional protections for citizens, their rights to give in charity, and their rights to not be harassed by the government without charge or be subjected to rendition were all cancelled. The entire community was fearful of the government.

The U.S. Congress rushed to pass the USA Patriot Act into law without serious considerations of potential abuses. In the week following 9/11, Amnesty International reported over 540 assaults on Arab Americans. The Council on American-Islamic Relations (CAIR) released a report that detailed the forms of assaults as hate mail and assaults on personal property, businesses, and mosques. Community centers and mosques were also burned and defaced. Teachers, classmates, and their parents taunted Arab children. Employers terminated Arab employees.

For many other Americans, the only marker of Arab identity was the facial features shown in film. As a result, Sikh, Mexican, and other Americans who fit the profile of olive skin, dark curly hair, and foreign accent were mistaken for Arabs and assaulted with impunity. This confusion caused fear and trepidation in many communities that had nothing to do with 9/11, including Arab American communities. CAIR further reported that over 60,000 Arab Americans had their civil rights infringed upon by government policies after 9/11.

The USA Patriot Act granted sweeping powers to domestic law enforcement and international intelligence agencies. Because civil liberties were trampled by this act, which is still in force, the civil liberties of all Americans were imperiled regardless of the good intentions of protecting society. Financial institutions used extreme interpretations of the act to justify blacklisting Arab and Muslim accounts and borrowing for the purpose of large purchases such as homes and cars. Much of the blacklisting was

President George W. Bush discusses the parameters of the Patriot Act, 2006. (White House)

done on the basis of names. Names common in the Arab world were placed on a watch list.

U.S. secretary of state Condoleezza Rice accepted torture and extraordinary rendition as tools for gaining information on future or current terrorist activities in the United States. A special registration program was introduced that ruined some businesses as Arabs were laid off, men were deported, and some families fled the United States. Needless to say, Arab Americans and all Muslims were almost paralyzed with fear. Yet some of the fear transformed community members.

Community Response to Intimidation

Christians, Jews, Hindus, and others began to protest what was happening to this targeted community, and Arabs found that they had allies in their protests over the demise of civil liberties. Activists and advocates of all kinds in every religious community were called to action in various arenas. Community representatives made their way to Capitol Hill, the usual spiritual nature of Friday sermons in Arab American houses of worship changed to promote integration and activism, and CAIR and the American Civil Liberties Union immediately protested infractions of civil liberties.

Twin forces of racism and intolerance led to new alliances between organizations such as the American-Arab Anti-Discrimination Committee and the Arab American Institute. Both of these organizations began to advocate for protection of civil liberties and constitutional rights. These groups were joined by the Conference on Civil Rights and the Asian American Justice Center. Arab American visibility was raised in positive ways as communities aligned with other communities fighting injustice, negative stereotypes, and discrimination. Yet, a clear strategy remained unclear.

Arab and Muslim organizations specifically focused on government policy emerged to research and survey the general American community's response to their presence. In 2002, the Institute for Social Policy and Understanding emerged. According to its mission statement, the institute "conducts objective, solution-seeking research" to educate Arab and Muslim communities on democracy and the aims of plural American existence. This research has produced a number of significant publications that survey the communities on their feelings and experiences and the larger community on its perceptions. Research has also included studies on sensitive topics such as divorce and education, which provides knowledge about the community.

Along with others emigrating from countries whose systems of governance are not democratic, Arabs and Muslims have had to learn and then begin to acclimate to the fast pace of the United States and its system of governance. Participation in issues of civil liberties and forming alliances with organizations has given a new and much-needed dimension to these once solely ethnic organizations. The initial interrogations of employees and management of charitable organizations have not ceased, but the manner of approach and encounter has changed somewhat because of the advocacy.

Military Encounters

Arabs, both Christian and Muslim, have also experienced harassment and discrimination in their jobs as members of the military. Arabs have been members of the military since World War I. The current political climate has warranted singling them out for harassment and discriminations along with verbal abuses. The armed forces did not pay attention to either the ethnic identity or immigration status of its recruits prior to the political focus on immigration and Arab Americans. Similarly, there have been Arab Americans in government for decades.

In *United States v. Hasan K. Akbar,* a U.S. Army soldier was court-martialed for a premeditated attack in the early morning hours of March

23, 2003, at Camp Pennsylvania, Kuwait, during the start of the U.S. invasion of Iraq. Born Mark Fidel Kools on April 21, 1971, Sergeant Hasan Karim Akbar allegedly threw four hand grenades into three tents in which other members of the 101st Airborne Division were sleeping. He also fired his rifle at fellow soldiers in the ensuing chaos. U.S. Army captain Christopher S. Seifert was fatally shot in the back during the chaos, and U.S. Air Force major Gregory L. Stone was killed by a grenade. Akbar wounded 14 other soldiers, mostly from grenade shrapnel.

At the trial, Akbar's military defense attorneys pointed to his psychiatric problems, including irrational behavior, paranoia, insomnia, and other sleep disorders. In April 2005, he was convicted and sentenced to death for the murders of Stone and Seifert. Akbar's sentence was affirmed by the Army Court of Criminal Appeals on July 13, 2012, and the U.S. Court of Appeals for the Armed Forces affirmed the decision on August 19, 2015. Though Akbar was an African American Muslim, he has come to represent both Arabness and the influences of the religion of Islam. In articles about this incident, the fact that he is a black American is the last of the descriptors. On the other hand, Arabs and Muslims read accounts of what other American soldiers were doing in Iraq, presumably in retaliation for 9/11 attacks. Arab American soldiers were in some of these battalions also.

At home in the United States, Americans understood implicitly that the armed forces had been on a mission of liberation and eradication of terrorism since President George W. Bush declared the war on terror. What was really happening in Iraq was reported by Arab media but not by American media until the leaking of the brutalities at Abu Ghraib prison. The *New Yorker* magazine reported in 2003 that

> The photographs tell it all. In one, Private England, a cigarette dangling from her mouth, is giving a jaunty thumbs-up sign and pointing at the genitals of a young Iraqi, who is naked except for a sandbag over his head, as he masturbates. Three other hooded and naked Iraqi prisoners are shown, hands reflexively crossed over their genitals. A fifth prisoner has his hands at his sides. In another, England stands arm in arm with Specialist Graner; both are grinning and giving the thumbs-up behind a cluster of perhaps seven naked Iraqis, knees bent, piled clumsily on top of each other in a pyramid. There is another photograph of a cluster of naked prisoners, again piled in a pyramid. Near them stands Graner, smiling, his arms crossed; a woman soldier stands in front of him, bending over, and she, too, is smiling. Then, there is another cluster of hooded bodies, with a female soldier standing in front, taking photographs. Yet another photograph shows a kneeling, naked, unhooded male prisoner, head momentarily turned away

from the camera, posed to make it appear that he is performing oral sex on another male prisoner, who is naked and hooded. (Hersh 2004)

America was embarrassed, while Arabs were humiliated and debased.

Those Arab Americans who had agreed with the invasion of Iraq and the removal of Saddam Hussein became invisible in the face of this humiliation. General rules of war apparently did not apply when it came to fighting Arabs in the Middle East, and with the USA Patriot Act, the rules of domestic civility and civil liberties were absent at home also. Unfortunately, the absence of strategies for response was glaringly absent here too. The Arab or Muslim community did not leverage these instances into a wider discussion about war in the 21st century.

Military encounters spawned uses of terms such as "enemy combatant" and "collateral damage" to cover other kinds of abuses. They were terrorists or associated with terrorists, so killing the innocent at weddings or funerals was incidental and not investigated. Arabs became fodder at home in the United States and abroad. Perhaps due to a lack of strategies, Arab Americans did come to partially understand the necessity of political participation.

Arab Americans in Government

Arab Americans serve in all levels of government from local offices to the U.S. Congress. There have been 17 Arab Americans over time serving in the U.S. Congress. Despite the turmoil of efforts regarding Palestinian solidarity advocacy, in the late 1980s the majority leader of the U.S. Senate was Arab American George Mitchell. By 1998, 6 U.S. representatives and 1 U.S. senator of Arab descent served their constituents and the government. Today, there are 7 U.S. representatives who are of Christian Arab American origin (6 are Republican, and 1, Gwen Graham, is a Democrat). As a group of mostly conservatives, they have deviated from their colleagues in voting against or cosponsoring bills that favored indefinite detention of prisoners at Guantánamo, for instance, and have supported the United States taking a leadership role in resolving Arab-Israeli issues.

That all are Republican except one is an interesting phenomenon. In 2000, Abu Dhabi Television commissioned Zogby International to poll randomly selected Arab American voters. The initial finding was that Arab Americans supported the candidacy of Republican George W. Bush over the candidacy of Democrat Al Gore by a margin of 45.5 percent to 38.8 percent. Green Party candidate Ralph Nader won 13.5 percent of the community's vote. Bush captured the support of 86.5 percent of all Arabs who registered Republican versus Al Gore, who got 75 percent of Arab American Democrats' votes.

Half of those who chose Bush over Gore said that their decision was based on the presence of Senator Joseph Lieberman, a Jew, on the Democratic ticket. They disagreed with his stance on the issues. Those who voted for Nader said that their decision was heavily influenced by his Arab American heritage. The conflict between Arabs and Israelis was escalating and significantly influenced Arab American voters moreso than domestic issues. Arab Americans were looking to have their views on U.S. Middle Eastern policy reflected.

Arab Americans respect the Republican Party values of a strong work ethic, conservative family social values, and adherence to religion. Republican support for lower taxes, smaller government, entrepreneurship, prolife movements, protection of traditional marriage, keeping and bearing arms, and safeguarding religious liberties is attractive to many Arab Americans. What is not so attractive and is increasingly alarming is Republicans' increasing hostility to Arabs and Muslims. In the 2016 election, Republicans led the way on banning people from Arab states from immigrating to the United States and have increased deportations in the very Christian communities they swore to protect.

Profiles

Steve Jobs (1955–2011) was an American entrepreneur, businessman, inventor, and industrial engineer who cofounded and chaired Apple Inc., which revolutionized communications with the iPhone. He was also a majority shareholder in Pixar.

Amos Muzyad Yakhoob Kairouz (1912–1991) was better known in his professional life as Danny Thomas. He was an American nightclub comedian, actor, singer, and producer for over five decades. He is the founder of St. Jude Children's Research Hospital, which opened its doors in 1962.

Edward Said (1935–2003) was a literature professor at Columbia University, a public intellectual, and a founder of the postcolonial studies academic field. He revolutionized many fields with his pioneering work *Orientalism*. In 1978, Professor Said exposed the Western representations of what they called the Orient, which was the Middle East, with "romance, exotic beings, haunting memories and landscapes" (Said 2014, 21). He drew correlations between European colonies from which they got their riches and the deprivations they left behind. This text continues to inspire and revolutionize many fields of study.

Donna Shalala (1941–) served as the U.S. secretary of health and human services from 1993 to 2001 under President Bill Clinton. From 2001 to 2015, she was president of the University of Miami.

References

Burch, Audra D. S. "He Became a Hate Crime Victim. She Became a Widow." *New York Times,* July 8, 2017, https://www.nytimes.com/2017/07/08/us/he-became-a-hate-crime-victim-she-became-a-widow.html.

Hersh, Seymour M. "Torture at Abu Ghraib." *New Yorker,* May 10, 2004, https://www.newyorker.com/magazine/2004/05/10/torture-at-abu-ghraib.

Maira, Sunaina Mara. *The 9/11 Generation: Youth, Rights, and Solidarity in the War on Terror.* New York: New York University Press, 2016.

Said, Edward W. *Orientalism.* 1978; reprint, New York: Knopf Doubleday, 2014.

Sirin, Selcuk R., and Michelle Fine. *Muslim American Youth: Understanding Hyphenated Identities through Multiple Methods.* New York: New York University Press, 2008.

"World Report 2001." Human Rights Watch, http://pantheon.hrw.org/legacy/wr2k1/.

CHAPTER NINE

Special Cases

Iraq and Syria

It was rather quickly established that the perpetrators of 9/11 were Arab and from Saudi Arabia and the United Arab Emirates. U.S. president George W. Bush attacked Afghanistan and then Iraq. Other simultaneous attacks on the nation's consciousness created an environment crippled with fear that made the attack on Iraq plausible. At first glance this war, which has now commanded attention for 16 years, was spur of the moment, impetuous, and ill-placed. The lead-up to this war actually began in 1999.

The Persian Gulf War (1990–1991) was hailed as a win for the United States, but in 1993 Saddam Hussein attempted to assassinate President George H. W. Bush as retaliation for his intervention in Iraq's war with Kuwait. By 1998, the Project for a New American Century (founded by Richard Cheney, Scooter Libby, Donald Rumsfeld, Jeb Bush, Paul Wolfowitz, and others) moved to persuade President Bill Clinton to undertake the removal of Hussein's regime. Al Qaeda, a predominantly Arab terrorist group, was active in the Middle East at this time and bombed U.S. embassies in Africa, killing 200 and injuring about 4,000 in 1998. By the end of 1998 President Clinton signed the Iraq Liberation Act, which made regime change official U.S. policy.

An Iraqi politician, Ahmed Chalabi, played a significant role in the lead-up to the 2003 invasion of Iraq. His group provided the intelligence upon which the United States relied, including reports of weapons of mass destruction in the hands of Hussein. Many wealthy Arab Americans agreed with the need to remove Hussein and saw his regime as increasingly hostile to the Iraqi people; the war with Kuwait was seen as a folly and proof of his insanity. Chalabi, who had studied at MIT and the University of Chicago, held a position of trust in the U.S. government despite rumors of his lack of integrity. Despite the insistence of Chalabi and others, it would take almost two years to garner enough support in Congress and among the American people for an attack on Iraq. And then 9/11 happened.

Most Arab Americans were terrified as they listened to the ramping up of anti-Arab sentiment that followed 9/11. Seven days after the attacks, the anthrax attacks on government offices began while President George W. Bush was still focused not on Al Qaeda but instead on Hussein. By September 21, 2001, Justice Department lawyer John Yoo declared that the Fourth Amendment of the U.S. Constitution was flexible and that the government could take measures to infringe on individual liberties. In early 2002 President Bush approved the program, which permitted the National Security Agency to surveil U.S. citizens without a warrant, court approval, or sign-off from the Justice Department. With terror alerts, detentions, and renditions, the United States invaded Iraq in 2003.

Arab Americans tried to become invisible. The goal of invading Iraq moved away from removing Hussein to liberating Shia Muslims from minority Sunni control to a need to prevent Iranian support for the Shia people the United States was liberating. Cultural markers of how religious difference had been managed for hundreds of years were buried, and contemporary opportunities for dominance took center stage. One Iraqi asserted that "Sect wasn't really a part of the national consciousness. I was born in Iraq and I'd never in my life been asked if I was a Sunni or a Shiite. And I didn't know who among my relatives or neighbors or co-workers or colleagues at school were Sunnis or Shiites, because it wasn't an issue. It's not that people were tolerant toward each other—they weren't aware of sectarian backgrounds. It's similar to some areas in the US where you don't necessarily know what Christian sect your friends belong to. You might know, or you might not know" (Moyers 2014).

It was reported that the U.S. attack in 2003 destroyed Iraqi national identity and replaced it with sectarian and ethnic identities. The promises of liberation, freedom, democracy, and rebuilding quickly evaporated. In the 1970s, Iraq was an Arab country governed largely by a secular philosophy. Fifty percent of its workforce were women, many schools and universities had been built, and scholarships were made available for women to study abroad for advanced degrees. Women were the hardest hit by the sanctions in the 1990s and in the 21st century. Immigration to the United States was slow, and by 2008 fewer than 10,000 received refugee status despite their work on behalf of the United States as soldiers and translators. The rise of the Islamic State of Iraq and Syria (ISIS), an offshoot of Al Qaeda, further decimated an already broken country. Today there are more than 200,000 Iraqi Americans still worrying about what will happen to their ancestral home and the relatives left behind.

An interview with one Iraqi American pinpoints the angst: Mr. Bahadli lives in Seattle, but his 5 brothers, 3 sisters, and 38 nieces and nephews remain in the Iraqi capital, which Mr. Bahadli left more than two decades ago. As forces aligned with ISIS ravaged his homeland over the previous week, he focused less on politics and more on those fleeing the fighting. "If you are a Christian, if you are a Muslim, if you are a Jew and you don't agree with their perspective, they call you a heathen and they kill you" (Schleifer 2014).

Also in the summer of 2014, CBS News reported on an Iraqi émigré's life in America. This particular person had been hired by CBS on the eve of the U.S. invasion as a photographer, translator, and expert on local knowledge. Soon labeled a collaborator, Atheer could not flee Iraq immediately but eventually landed in Lancaster, Pennsylvania. Although he had a college degree, he worked in a chicken-processing plant and as a school janitor. It did not matter that his photographs were famous. CBS News found him again after the story about him ran, and KYW-TV in Philadelphia hired him as a cameraman. One happy ending in a sea of woe.

While support for the invasion of Iraq ran as high as 46 percent in 2003, support has dwindled steadily downward to 75 percent of Americans feeling that it was not worth it. The cost in human lives on both sides (including the permanently wounded) has been too great with little gain. When President Donald Trump asserted that he would defeat ISIS by taking over the oil fields the terrorists have seized in Iraq, Arab and many other Americans gasped in horror. After all, the United States invaded Iraq, but the terrorists did not come from Iraq.

Despite the copious amounts of government money poured into Middle Eastern study programs, the U.S. government still struggles to understand the cultures and politics of the Middle East. Scholarship that did not agree with government positions was sidelined, while a slew of "experts" and institutes arose whose political interests against anything but superficial explanations of the situation ruled the day.

Anti-Arab and anti-Muslim organizations have produced a new revenue stream in the world of pseudoexpertise in Islam, Muslim cultures, and politics along with terrorism and hate-mongering. Members of these groups have fashioned themselves as genuinely concerned for the well-being of America and as watchdogs for Arabs and Muslims attempting to subvert the quality of life in the country. The Fox News channel has been one of their broadcast homes, and millions of Americans tune in to get the latest analysis of international, national, and local news.

A Federal Bureau of Investigation internal memo obtained by the independent news research group Public Intelligence reported that extremist and armed American militia groups were planning a campaign of violence targeting Muslim and Arab institutions such as mosques and schools (Hanania 2017). Members of these various groups have considered beheadings, kidnappings, arson, and outright killings in retaliation for the atrocities perpetrated by ISIS on American citizens in the Middle East. Tragically, some congresspersons, local politicians, and news outlets are supporting these groups. Arab Americans have been in the United States for over 100 years and have made small and large contributions to its democracy and continued growth. The events overseas, however, have overshadowed their roots and made them liable for the acts of criminals and vagaries of war. Arabs and Muslims in the United States are held accountable for every act of war or atrocity in the Middle East by proxy. By default, all Arabs are Muslim, and all Muslims are Arab. There is little distinction made between Arab Christian victims of Arab Muslim violence and little recognition of intermarrying between the two groups. This is really no different than the animus between blacks and whites in the United States and their continuous intermarrying.

Reflecting on the Al Qaeda attacks of September 11, 2001, scholar Yvonne Haddad asserted that

> the questions that future scholars will have to investigate include whether the attacks had a lasting effect on Arabs and Muslims and their integration and assimilation in the United States, as well as what permanent impact, if any, they will have on the unfolding of the articulation of Islam in the American public square. (Haddad 2011, 1)

Today in 2018, these questions still have relevance and cannot be answered even partially.

Syria

Official relations between the United Sates and Syria began in 1835 with an appointment of U.S. consuls to Aleppo in the Ottoman Empire. The United States recognized an independent Syria in 1946. The Central Intelligence Agency attempted a coup in 1957 (unsuccessful) against President Shukri al-Quwatli and withdrew the U.S. ambassador. Relations were not restored until 1974 following the signing of the Israeli-Syrian Separation of Forces Agreement.

During the Persian Gulf War (1990–1991), Syria cooperated with the United States against Iraq. Though relations began to cool following the attacks of 9/11 and Syria's provision of only limited intelligence to the United States on the movements of Al Qaeda, Syria has become one of the destinations for U.S. renditions of enemy combatants. Nevertheless, Syria is considered a secular dictatorship with an abysmal human rights record. It has been on the list of states that sponsor terrorism since 1979, though it has not been directly associated with terrorist attacks for decades. Yet as a part of its amassing of an army, ISIS took up residence alongside a number of other revolutionary and government resistant groups. The United States has issued seven executive orders that impose sanctions on certain Syrian citizens or entities due to their participation in terrorism, acts of public corruption, or destabilizing activities in Iraq and Lebanon. By 2011 President Barack Obama had frozen all assets of the government of Syria and prohibited U.S. persons from any transaction involving that government. From 2006 through 2010, the United States issued a travel advisory for American citizens traveling to Syria, hampering the efforts of family visits and wellness checks. With a new administration came new problems: "During and after his campaign, President Trump proposed establishing safe zones in Syria as an alternative to Syrian refugees" immigrating to the United States (Ainsley and Spetalnick 2017). This has resulted in attempts at a full ban.

The Syrian American Council has as its stated mission and vision to be the leading grassroots Syrian American organization advocating for freedom and democracy in Syria. As the first Arab immigrants to the United States over 100 years ago, Syrians have a colorful history here. They too are religiously and ethnically diverse. They are Arabs, Christians, Armenians, Assyrians, Jews, and Kurds, to name a few. They currently comprise about 12 percent of the Arab American population.

Researchers note that many of the first Arab Christians from Syria were peddlers who integrated by quickly learning English and making strenuous efforts at cultural contact. With Anglicized names, acculturation of English-language skills, and adoption of popular Christian denominations by many, they assimilated. Like other Arabs, Syrians in America shied away from political and civic life, preferring invisibility.

Though the first immigrants may have been peddlers, opportunities for higher education have led to a fairly wealthy community of professionals. According to the 2000 census, 42 percent of Syrian Americans worked in management and professional occupations, compared with 34 percent of all Americans. There are over 4,000 Syrian physicians practicing in every branch of medicine, representing 0.4 percent of the health care workforce. Their median household income is higher than that of other Arabs and Americans overall.

The sheer diversity of professions and career choices lends credence to the saying that immigrants make this nation great. Though Syrians have been forced to be invisible because of political winds, their creative talents have been on display for decades. It is increasingly difficult to see the struggle of the democratic experiment in the United States, especially given the fact that the openness that was expected is no longer there (Haddad 2011). For many Arab Americans, the hypocrisy runs deep and is abiding. The United States has long represented itself as the democratic freedom-loving example of civil liberties at its best. As the country toggles between leading the world and becoming isolationist in its dealings, the impetus grows to place the anger on vulnerable populations: Arab Americans and a recaptured animus against blacks, Latinos, and anyone else who decries white supremacy. How scholars, researchers, and other investigators answer Haddad's question about the effects of 9/11 on Arab American populations remains unknown, but the feelers are out from this community as to how to invisibly further weave itself into the nation's fabric and simultaneously make its voice heard when the suspicion and unfair treatment is too much. Perhaps a further question is how other Americans are going to trod the path of reconciliation in the persistent face of ongoing chaos, racism, and discrimination. The more time it takes to heal, the more the wounds will fester. Arab Americans are not going anywhere.

Profiles

Paula Abdul (June 19, 1962–) is a multiplatinum Grammy Award–winning singer, Emmy Award–winning choreographer, television personality, and jewelry designer. Abdul has sold over 53 million records. She found renewed fame as a judge on the highly rated television series *American Idol*.

Mitch Daniels (April 7, 1949–) is a former governor of Indiana (2005–2013) and the current president of Purdue University.

Hala Gorani (March 1, 1970–) is a news anchor and correspondent for CNN International.

Sam Yagan (1977–) is an American entrepreneur, business executive, and cofounder of SparkNotes, eDonkey, OkCupid, and Techstars Chicago as well as the CEO of Match Group, which owns Tinder.

References

Ainsley, Julia Edwards, and Matt Spetalnick. "Trump Says He Will Order 'Safe Zones' for Syria." *Reuters,* January 25, 2017, https://www.reuters.com /article/us-usa-trump-syria-safezones-idUSKBN1592O8.

Haddad, Yvonne. *Becoming American? The Forging of Arab and Muslim Identity in Pluralist America.* Waco, TX: Baylor University Press, 2011.

Hanania, Ray. "Right Wing Militias Targeting Mosque and Muslim Groups." *Arab Daily News,* August 10, 2017.

Moyers, Bill. "An Iraqi Perspective: How America's Destruction of Iraqi Society Led to Today's Chaos." Moyers and Company, June 20, 2014, https://bill moyers.com/2014/06/20/an-iraqi-perspective-how-americas-destruction -of-iraqi-society-led-to-todays-chaos/.

Schleifer, Theodore. "Iraqi-Americans Watch Chaos in Alarm." *New York Times,* June 21, 2014.

CHAPTER TEN

Arab Americans Post–9/11

In the aftermath of September 11, 2001, the U.S. government unleashed a series of unprecedented legal strategies that curtailed the religious and civil liberties of Arab Americans. In doing so, the government also restricted the civil liberties of all Americans. This chapter will explore those societal changes and restrictions and their effects on the lives of Arab Americans. It is important to first explore very briefly the legal history of religious communities and the state.

Issue of Church and State

The issues surrounding religious liberty and the role of religion in this democratic experiment are profound concerning Arab Americans after 9/11. The role of religious liberty in a democratic society is a question that has plagued the United States since its inception and continues to play a part as the diversity of the country grows more complicated. Courts have ruled differently at various times regarding the interaction of church and state. Attempting to determine the correct relationship between church and state—or among law, religion, and government—has historically been an uphill battle.

The Jehovah's Witnesses have led many of the battles revolving around the separation of church and state. For example, in *Minersville School District v. Gobitis* (1940), parents sued because their children were expelled from public school for refusing on religious grounds to recite the Pledge of Allegiance to the American flag. The judge in this case insisted that the state could not seek to coerce "children to express a sentiment which violates their deepest religious conviction." This ruling affirmed the separation

Linda Sarsour (right), Program Director for the Arab American Association. (Robert Nickelsberg/Getty Images)

of church and state and was not challenged again until the efforts of the Moral Majority in the 1980s.

The Pledge of Allegiance has its own history. During the 1880s and 1890s when the pledge was written by Francis Bellamy, labor conditions were terrible, unions had not yet gained strength, and wealthy monopolies were still legal. In addition to these social conditions, immigrants were pouring into the country. There were raging debates over first the universality of public education and then over the funding for public and parochial schools. The American Civil War had just ended, and the country was still healing. The pledge was created to be a soothing balm. By the time of the *Gobitis* litigation, it had become standard fare in public schools across the nation.

Even though this chapter focuses on post–9/11, Arab American problems in U.S. society escalated after the Iran hostage crisis in 1979. This crisis, although having nothing to do with Arabs, became an issue for Arabs, since Americans had no idea what an Iranian looked like; Arab Americans became stand-in Iranians. Arab American Muslim women's scarves were pulled off their heads in public spaces, some Arab Americans lost their jobs or were prevented from enrolling in colleges and universities, and children were harassed in schools across the nation.

The Council on American-Islamic Relations (CAIR) was founded in 1994 with an express commitment to ensure that the rights given to every citizen are enforced for citizens of the Islamic faith. Before 9/11, CAIR found itself tested as a nascent civil rights organization. Muslim citizens, predominantly Arabs, sought relief from egregious attacks on their persons and property. Finally, there was a place to register a complaint.

One of the first complaints to CAIR resulted from an incident in 1998 when seven white men approached a husband and wife who were picnicking in a Chicago-area forest preserve, recognizing them as Muslim because of the wife's scarf. One of the men exposed himself and urinated in front of the couple and then, with a string of profanities about their being terrorists, threatened with the police present to rape the wife and beat and sexually assault the husband. The men assumed that the police would be on their side, and the officers made no attempt to intervene or arrest. The men were not arrested.

September 11, 2001

The horrific events of 9/11 were committed by Saudi Arabs, all from the Middle East and members of the Islamic faith. Airplane travel was seriously curtailed, and new rules for travel and surveillance were enacted. President George W. Bush signed the USA Patriot Act into law on October 26, 2001. This act was designed to provide the appropriate tools required to intercept and obstruct acts of terrorism on U.S. soil.

The USA Patriot Act authorized law enforcement to use surveillance against potential further acts of terror. The act allowed federal agents to track suspected terrorists, allowed law enforcement to search and seize without warning, and allowed federal agents to obtain business records in suspected national security terrorism cases. Immigration officials fingerprinted, photographed, and interviewed some 85,000 Muslim and Arab noncitizens from November 2002 to May 2003, hoping to hunt down terrorists (Swarns 2003). Other immigrants were exempted from this requirement.

Arab and Muslim charities were pounced upon by many government agencies including the Internal Revenue Service, which immediately claimed that they were sources of support for terrorist groups. Arab and Muslim citizens were put on a wide-ranging no-fly list, ironically including former U.S. vice president Al Gore. Little could be done to change their status without vast sums of money and powerful influence. Since the act opened Guantánamo Prison and permitted the use of torture to extract information, a new regime of law enforcement was introduced. Arabs and Muslims now felt as though they had never been citizens.

Since the USA Patriot Act has never been revoked, many law enforcement agencies continued to exploit its excesses in an enduring persecution of Arabs in America. In New York City and in several surrounding cities, the police began to dub mosques as terrorist hubs, and students belonging to either Arab or Muslim student groups were deemed suspicious. Paid informants became a staple of Federal Bureau of Investigation (FBI) and Central Intelligence Agency operations. Documentaries such as *Terror* featured informants who exposed some of these operations. Men who did not belong to a community were instructed to act as "converts" to the religion in order to attend regular Friday prayers and classes. These informants were highly paid, which also provided incentives for some men who were members of communities to falsify scenarios of potential danger to suit their handlers. The communities themselves felt under siege.

Secondary Security Screening Selection (the no-fly list) was created after September 11, 2001, along with the selectee list and the terrorist watchlist, by the Bush administration to protect the nation. Tens of thousands of names wound up on the no-fly list, while millions filled the terrorist watchlist. It was not until 2015 that citizens could find out why they were on the list and dispute the classification. The dragnet that these lists created swept up large numbers of ordinary citizens and violated the Fifth Amendment rights of all.

Arab and Muslim Americans now felt an acute need to gain allies, and they found quite a few. The American Civil Liberties Union began its fight against the lists early. Other faith groups saw the overreaction to Arabs and Muslims as an assault against the First Amendment and sought to add their voices to protests. Activists of varying ranks, including the National Security Agency, began early to protest the increasing lists of racial and religious discriminations. Arab and Muslim organizations began tentative outreach efforts and were rewarded with new alliances. Yet the angst never cooled, and neither did the efforts at surveillance. The rhetoric, undefined and then refined, focused itself on terrorism, fear, and hatred.

Terrorism

Formal definitions of terrorism often leave out its arbitrariness and brutality for the sake of brutality without political gain, as in cases such as domestic violence. Yet arbitrariness is such a prominent feature of the kind of violence represented by the events of 9/11. The various industries and economies formed by uses of terrorism were, however, quite deliberate.

Americans were introduced to the phrases "illegitimate violence," "nonstate actors," and "Islamic extremism" almost simultaneously. Bush's war on terrorism coupled with his rhetoric of "for us or against us" cemented a narrative that grew to unimaginable proportions. Terrorism became a staple of news coverage. Audiences had to be taught how to view what they were seeing but only after the government and its supporters figured out what the lens was.

Audiences interpret information through varied lenses: class, race, ethnicity, religion, and even varied experiences of terror/violence. Scriptwriters, authors, and so on aimed to get as many aspects of American society on the same page as possible regarding the war on terrorism. Movies and TV shows portrayed undertrained counterterrorism agents who either killed the wrong person or fell in love with the Arab terrorist and became a traitor. In movies such as *Unthinkable,* viewers are witness to the overtrained counterterrorism agent/resident psychopath who has seen so much terror and participated in so many interrogations that he is sadistic. While moviegoers and television watchers were either horrified or entertained, they were also being lulled into the paralyzing effect of terror.

Under the rhetorical banner of "for us or against us," research, news reports, etc., became surveilled for compliance or sedition. Patriotism (symbolized by flags on porches and lawns of homes, lapels of suits, and car windows) and national unity (perpetually on display by the military bands of the armed forces at sports games and other national events) became the new national order. Academia became a target for surveillance, since Arab students had small student groups on campuses across the country. Professors of civil rights, liberal theories, and political science would critique the antics of terrorism.

Groups such as the Middle East Forum, founded by Professor Daniel Pipes, whom critics claimed to be pro-Israeli, paid students to attend and disrupt classes on Middle Eastern studies in asserted efforts to improve them. In online scholarly forums, it was reported that professors who took at least neutral but sometimes positive stances toward Arab points of view were labeled sympathizers, run out of jobs, and blackballed by publishers in efforts reminiscent of the McCarthy era. One such professor, Larycia Hawkins, found herself out of a job and out of a Christian community in Wheaton, Illinois. Faculties sought to protect themselves from extinction by forgoing academic freedoms, and classrooms became quiet without academic exchange. Institutional censorship and self-censorship again became the order of the day.

The narrative surrounding terrorism began to build its grammar in the months after 9/11. Only nonstate (nongovernmental) actors committed acts of terror. The majority of the terrorist groups were Arab or Arab-affiliated. Terrorism (not poverty or income disparities) is the major threat to civilization and is caused by radicalization. Terrorism became a closed knowledge system with its own experts, many of whom had never been to the Middle East and were groomed from other jobs or disciplines.

Middle Eastern specialists who were either religiously or culturally Muslim found themselves censored and self-censoring. In order to continue in academic or diplomatic posts, they had to prove themselves patriotic beyond a doubt. An additional industry was spawned around that of the culture-hating Arab. Even though many of their grievances with the societies of ancestors were most times real, these grievances came to underscore and affirm the old adages about Arabs and the backward and illegitimate religion of Islam.

The narrative of 9/11 evolved into a system of knowledge that required commemoration of "national trauma." American victims became more innocent and more significant than any other victims of terror anywhere in the world. These Arab terrorists were different from other terrorists; their methods were equally unique, and above all, some of them were living among us. Arabs who are radicalized or who self-radicalize from pleas on websites are threatening American liberty, freedom, justice, and democracy—they hate our freedoms. These terrorists were not just killing people; they were attacking values.

Just as external events in the Middle East persistently challenged and sometimes changed Arab American articulated identity, the events of 9/11 forever changed American identity. Every society has idealized notions of what their values are, and America is no exception. Usually the process of identity building starts with what a particular group is not. Americans are not aboriginal peoples, not of enslaved African ancestry, not descendants of Ottomans, and not terrorists. All American violence against individuals or states is legitimate, though it could be wrong. The victims of American violence were not innocent victims but rather "collateral damage" (Hedges 2009, xxiii).

Finally, terrorism has become a significant dimension of religious life and the retail market. Its definition, causes, and descriptions of its proponents are in study books and religious magazines and on television programs and are even aspects of some sermons. Designers producing protective clothing and apps for mobile phones have multiplied exponentially to assuage the fears of an increasingly violent America. Much of this violence is directed toward citizens, naturalized or born, of Middle Eastern heritage or a heritage that resembles it.

Sharia

Issues of religious faith have always found their way into America's courtrooms. Given the multireligious and philosophical natures of citizens in the early centuries of the nation, even the question of how to ensure that the truth is being heard became a religious issue. For those who believed in the Bible and its promises of future rewards for truth telling and punishments for lying, swearing on the Bible to tell the truth gave the courts some comfort. Those who did not believe in the Bible were deemed unqualified to provide testimony by the courts. Truth telling was tied to religious belief. Immediately challenges arose. In the 19th and early 20th centuries when a defendant was asked to testify but did not believe in the Bible and was found guilty, how were rights maintained for that person without his or her taking an oath to tell the truth? What happens when the litigants believe in the future promises of another sacred text? It was not until the middle of the 20th century that other sacred texts were permitted in the oath process.

Three world religions (Judaism, Catholic Christianity, and Islam) have religious laws that inform the life of believers. Believers are born, marry, and have death rituals all under the guidance of these laws. U.S. courts hold as valid religious marriages, though divorces require state intervention because of property and child custody issues. When claims about specifically domestic issues and sometimes issues of death go to court, it is not at all unusual for religious laws to be invoked. For example, Judaism and Islam prohibit some actions on dead bodies and require that the dead be buried within 24 hours if possible. Religious litigants have used religious obligations as testimony throughout American history, as court records attest. Of course, religious bodies grant exceptions to religious laws when the needs of the state take precedence, such as in murder cases, and no religious law supersedes U.S. law.

After September 11, 2001, the use of Islamic law in courts began to draw ire. Though a few Muslim litigants referred to Islamic law as justification for actions, judges used those references in the same way that they consider family situations or mental illnesses—as part of evaluating the individual situation. Some lawmakers, however, began to mount a campaign suggesting that Muslims were using their religious law as a strategy to make all citizens adhere to it and thus take over America. Though this suggestion was absurd, it gained enormous traction after 9/11. States began to pass referendums aimed specifically at prohibiting any mention of Islamic law. Only a few of these referendums were passed, though the fear they represented spread across the country, with Oklahoma and Tennessee leading the way.

In November 2010, citizens of the state of Oklahoma were asked to consider State Question 755, called the "Save our State" constitutional amendment. The foundation for the question emerged from a case in New Jersey's family court involving a Muslim woman who asked for a restraining order against her husband for repeatedly raping her. The husband's defense was that he was following his religious beliefs regarding spousal duties and relations. The judge sided with the husband. Though the judgment was later overturned in appellate court, the fact that Islamic law could even be considered in an American court ruling sparked outrage. Further, the possibility that a judge could apply Islamic legal rulings to non-Muslims was put on the floor for debate. More concern was raised when Elena Kagan said in her 2010 confirmation hearing that as a justice for the U.S. Supreme Court she would be willing to consider international law when listening to cases before the court.

Despite the sensationalism that erupted from the New Jersey case and Kagan's comments, religious courts and tribunals operated in the United States throughout much of the 20th century and into the 21st century. The Federal Arbitration Act of 1925 permitted Muslims, Christians, Jews, and others who follow religious law to use religious tribunals to arbitrate disagreements; judgments stemming from them had the force of state and federal courts.

This act preempted inconsistent state legislation on issues such as Islamic Law. For Jews, Beth Din (Rabbinical Court) was established to arbitrate between devout Jews (Orthodox). The Roman Catholic Church has nearly 200 diocesan tribunals to handle a variety of Catholic issues. It was expected that Muslims would have teams of Islamic scholars from various schools of thought to handle their issues. All religious persons in these communities have the option to get relief in secular courts, although Orthodox Jews must have permission of the Rabbinical Court.

The Federal Arbitration Act did not just emerge from out of the blue; it has its origin in treaties and laws binding European states. As Europe was forming itself as a cohesive unit instead of a host of totally independent countries, the need for some internal coherence emerged. Notions of sovereignty and a community of countries with similar morals, manners, and understandings of humanity evolved. A system of rules was put in place along with guidelines for forming alliances and treaties—the essence of international law.

The very nature of conflict between European states was religion, and the negotiation of this conflict became one significant aspect of international law. A system of rules was devised, called the code of public law, consisting of laws that "regulate the structure and administration of the government, the conduct of the government in its relations with its citizens, the responsibilities of government employees and the relationships with foreign governments" (Duhaime's Law Dictionary). Overwhelmingly Christian, the rules found their affirmation in biblical understandings. Though the United States fought its way out of the British Empire, it kept the rules, which later found an appropriate expression regarding religious affairs in the Federal Arbitration Act of 1925.

This history and its rationale have never found their way into the current debates over the use of or reference to Islamic law. Even the existence of religious courts in faith communities has not been a part of the discussion. Assertions that Islamic law somehow applies to non-Muslims defies Islamic history, and the very thought that its users intend to supplant the law of the land is both anti-Islamic and unconstitutional. Some scholars think that the hostilities of the days of the Ottoman Empire and the Barbary Coast skirmishes remain active in the subconscious and that film, television, and books have reawakened that consciousness of fear and potential terror. Remarkably, the perpetrators are still seen as Arab, though the visual aspects of Arab have changed.

The diverse roots of Arab Americans have not mattered much on the American landscape. They have been melded into one people by language, media, and 9/11. The Arab world is the world of Islam even though it is also the home of Judaism and Christianity. The current wave of terrorism is cast as Arab-initiated and Islam-inspired. Utterances in Arabic by perpetrators since 9/11 asserting that their acts are in the name of God further connect the Arabic language to terrorism. The fact that most Arab Americans continue to be Christian is of little account, as the thrust of counterterrorist efforts is against all Arabs, who have been further identified as Muslims and perpetrators of Islamist terrorism. The fear of Arabs and Islam that has been instilled has resulted in another construction: Islamophobia.

Islamophobia

Fear of Islamic takeover due to the presence of Muslims on American soil has become entrenched in the minds of some everyday citizens and politicians. This fear has led to persistent criminal acts against Muslims and their homes and houses of worship. Muslim women who cover their heads have been attacked in grocery stores and on the streets, fires have been set at mosques, and attempts have been made to firebomb stores

Muslim Americans protest against war and Islamophobia. (Mario Tama/Getty Images)

thought to be owned by Muslims. Most recently, the government attempted to ban Muslims from entering the country from seven Muslim-majority states and succeeded in a partial ban. These efforts persist in several guises; the most prevalent one is the extreme vetting of Muslim travelers. This construction of Arabs, Muslims, Islam, and fear has its place in the hierarchy of enemies who must be fought at home and abroad.

Interestingly, "anti-Arabism" is definitionally distinct from "Islamophobia," though the two terms are often situationally, politically, and socially treated as synonyms. Given the history of relationships between America and the Middle East, the conflation of terms and attitudes is clear. North African and European experiences with successful and not so successful attempts at Arabization in the 14th and 15th centuries have remained a part of the collective memory. A subsequent hatred of Arabs, resulting in attempts at genocide in Spain and southern France, are also a part of that collective memory and came to America with the colonists. While the terms "anti-Arabism" and "Islamophobia" seem straightforward and separate, the experience of their full weight is felt dramatically in the Arab American community.

Prominent Arab non-Muslim communities feel the daily pressures associated with their names and ancestral points of origin. Many have shortened or changed their names, expanded their footprints into the larger societal structure, and in some cases become favorites on television and so on. This, however, has not altered the general understanding of the ambiguity of the terms of fear and hatred. While the diversity of roots should have a prominent hand in assisting understandings of these cultural groups linked by language and geography, it is obscured by politics.

Islamophobia is directly linked to the events of 9/11, even though it was present in later decades of the 20th century. Initially the horrific acts of 9/11 were labeled criminal, but quickly the labeling changed to acts of terror. There were significant spikes in Islamophobia and anti-Arab sentiments after 9/11 but remarkably also more than a decade later from 2014 to 2017. Most notably, after the election of Donald Trump as president and subsequent to the rhetoric of his campaign against Muslims and bans on some Arab countries, the spikes rose higher.

In 2013, a Carnegie Mellon University study found that nationally Muslims had 13 percent fewer callbacks than Christians after submitting identical job applications to the same establishments. This rejection was largely based on names. It is also concluded that many Arab Christians were put in the pool with Arab Muslims and denied because of name. This study also found that the percentage of denials was larger in counties with a high faction of Republican voters. In counties with a majority of Democratic voters, there was no discernible discrimination.

Between 2001 and 2009, the U.S. Equal Employment and Opportunity Commission (EEOC) reported a significant increase in claims of bias. The report actually stated that there "is hatred, an open hatred, and a lack of tolerance for workers who are Muslim" (*NBC Nightly News* 2010). This requires some effort on the part of employers to have a rubric for determination of who is Muslim. If only Arab names are identified, then the diverse roots of Arab Americans are hidden. If only Arab names are identified, then the majority of Muslims are misidentified. If some other means of identification is used (such as appearance), then Sikhs, persons of Hispanic descent, and others are rounded up in the mix. The arbitrariness of any rubric is problematic and has resulted in numerous potential court actions.

In their book *Islamophobia,* Peter Gottschalk and Gabriel Greenberg assert that "American popular interest in Muslims moved from the incidental interactions and clashes in the nineteenth century to conflicts Americans considered endemic in the twentieth and twenty-first centuries" (Gottshalk and Greenberg 2008, 37). The concerns that drew American attention to the Middle East (such as economic interests in oil, some religious concerns over the creation of the State of Israel, and global strategic alliances) made encounters with Middle Eastern populations more frequent. This put the Middle East, in the minds of many American scholars in public policy and international affairs, as a place of potential contention. This attention, however, did not did not revolve around issues of religion; rather, the focus was on nationalism and policy. The Middle East was not at the time connected to issues about the Muslim world. In the middle of the 20th century, the Middle East was the place of the movies—sand dunes, barely clothed women, and licentious men. It wasn't until the first oil embargo that Americans began to pay attention to what enabled them to live a life of gasoline luxury.

Even though the world's Jewish population has been trying for centuries to live in peace with others in the world, the assault on this population, especially by those who held them liable for the death of Jesus Christ, continuously put them in peril. When given an opportunity to consider a Jewish state, several places were discussed—even those as unconnected as Madagascar. Yet even before World War I, Palestine was only one area of interest. When the British mandate was established in Palestine in 1922 and a negotiation was entered into for a Jewish national home, Palestine was still not the only place considered. The criticality of finding a safe home for Jews became the world's problem after the Holocaust. America, though hesitant to take in Jews on its own shores, supported the establishment of the State of Israel, unmatched in tenacity by any other nation.

Scholars have given many reasons why America's support for Israel has always been so high. Israel is in a strategic location, as it is a democracy in a sea of monarchies and military states. Though socialist in many of its policies, it is not a communist or socialist state. The first major and continuing issue arose as governors of the State of Israel attempted to rescue Jews from oppressive situations around the world. Their relocation in Israel necessarily meant the relocation of many Arabs out of Israel. For Arabs, this aspect of the conflict became more Islamic with the Israeli capture of the Temple Mount/al-Aqsa Mosque in 1967 and the rise of the Palestine Liberation Organization. Although Arab Christians had little interest in the mosque, they did have intense interest in saving their churches and homes. The four outright wars fought contesting ownership of land made "terrorism" an everyday word in this part of the world and an "over there" word for many Americans.

After 9/11, political cartoonists such as Jack Ohman, Paul Conrad, Jeff Danziger, and Glenn McCoy elaborated on the symbols of Islam as symbols of difference. The sword became the way that Muslims deal with conflict; the Taliban flag was draped on the walls of mosques, and the phrase "you have to destroy a city and its people to save it" became popular. These cartoonists brought back the worst of the stereotypes of Arab sheikhs, oil barons, and fully covered women with heightened sexual appetites. The West was painted as angelic, moral, and freedom-loving, while the Middle East was again the place of the movies. Nevertheless, it was the oil embargo of 1973 that refashioned the hordes of Arab men and sandy dunes into a massive horde living in Arab states, acting as one to disenfranchise the West of a precious commodity. Little thought was given to whether they were Christian or Muslim—they were Arab.

In the conclusion of *Islamophobia,* Gottschalk and Greenberg recount a special episode of the hit TV series *The West Wing* in which

> a technical expert working in the White House comes under the sharp-edged suspicion of the chief of staff who harshly interrogates him, already convinced that the man, a Muslim, conspires with terrorists. When proven wrong the chief of staff proffers an awkward apology as the expression of the screenwriter's moral lesson that we must be careful about stereotypes. Indeed, as this, the last scene in the episode, fades to black, the Vietnam era Buffalo Springfield song "For What It's Worth" emphasizes the point with his cautionary lyrics of fear instilled and sides taken. (Gottschalk and Greenberg 2008, 143)

This scholar goes on to note that in all the previous episodes of this long-running TV series of seven years, Jews and Catholics were quite visible, but there were no Muslim characters until the special episode. It was only when it was safe to present the Muslim as a threat that such an episode could be aired.

Trump's tweets about Islam and Muslims after he became the Republican nominee for president certainly fueled Islamophobia. In June 2016 he issued a warning, without evidence, that his presumptive Democratic rival Hillary Clinton wanted radical Islamic terrorists to pour into our country. The *Washington Post* asserted that "Trump professed support for law-abiding Muslim Americans but said that if they didn't report on 'bad' people within their midst, 'these people have to have consequences, big consequences'" (Ignatius 2016). During an interview on *60 Minutes,* Trump then said that he was going to look into how to get rid of them when he became president.

By January 2017, Huffington Post could list 78 recorded incidents against mosques in 2015. Today that number has almost tripled, as has the number of assaults and attempted murders of Muslim men and women presumed to be tied to the Arab world. Trump warns that radical Muslims are trying to take over our children and has again succeeded in partially banning Arab Muslims from six countries from entry into the United States.

Profile

Muneer Awad (1973–) is the Palestinian American former executive director of the Oklahoma and New York City chapters of CAIR who led the fight against State Question 755 in Oklahoma. Awad was the plaintiff aiming to block the amendment on the grounds that it would make Oklahoma's constitution a vehicle for "enduring condemnation" of Islam.

References

Ariens, Michael, and Robert Desto. *Religious Liberty in a Pluralistic Society.* Durham, NC: Carolina Academic Press, 2002.

Duhaime's Law Dictionary. Duhaime.org.

Gottschalk, Peter, and Gabriel Greenberg. *Islamophobia: Making Muslims the Enemy.* Lanham, MD: Rowman and Littlefield, 2008.

Hallaq, Wael. *Introduction to Islamic Law.* Cambridge: Cambridge University Press, 2009.

Hedges, Chris. *Collateral Damage: America's War against Iraqi Civilians.* New York: Nation Books, 2009.

Ignatius, David. "Trump's Reckless, Dangerous Islamophobia Helps the Islamic State." *Washington Post,* June 13, 2016.

Jackson, Richard, et al. *Terrorism: A Critical Introduction.* New York: Palgrave/Macmillan, 2011.

Kamali, Mohammad Hashim. *Shari'ah Law: An Introduction.* London: Oneworld Publications, 2008.

Minersville School District v. Gobitis, 310 U.S. 586 1940.

NBC Nightly News. September 13, 2010.

Swarns, Rachel L. "Special Registration for Arab Immigrants Will Reportedly Stop." *New York Times,* November 22, 2003, http://www.nytimes.com /2003/11/22/us/special-registration-for-arab-immigrants-will-report edly-stop.html.

CHAPTER ELEVEN

Challenges to the Arab American Community in the 21st Century

Challenges to the Arab American community in the 21st century are daunting ones because of the events at the end of the 20th century and the beginning of the 21st century and, at the same time, the familiar continuing trials of fully integrating into a society that persists in finding almost everything about the community a threat. Integration of Arab Americans into American society has always been tempered by the status of Middle Eastern situations. The 21st century, beginning with the horrific events of 9/11, has set a tone that will undoubtedly last for the rest of the century.

The Middle East is composed of countries and cultures as different as those in Turkey, Yemen, Iran, Pakistan, and Oman. While at one time it was thought that everyone in the Middle East spoke Arabic, it is now known that there are many languages in the Middle East and that Arabic may even be a tertiary language of some people. Given that the people in each of these countries have their own issues with each other, the prospects for peace between them are slim. They occupy at least seven major cities for transportation of goods across one portion of the world, giving a heavy weight to their strategic global importance even in the encroaching era of cyberspace.

The oil reserves in this part of the world are still enormous, as are other mineral reserves such as lithium. The region and its geopolitical arrangement make it one of the most sought-after markets in the entire world,

Demonstrators protesting the travel ban in the United States, 2018. (Byron Smith/Getty Images)

with access to all global markets. As the Middle East signs onto digital transformation, the protection of that budding cybersecurity network becomes important for the world. Today the Middle Eastern region is home to the world's biggest oil and gas platforms, banking institutions, telecom giants, world-class airlines, and industrial control systems. To handle the needed infrastructure, Arabs have had to hire from all over the world. The best engineers, the best technicians, and the best thinkers are needed to join the global economic community. What Arab Americans see is that the world they left—because of an absence of opportunity and, for some, individual repression—is now a world full of opportunity though controlled again largely by someone else.

Since many Arab immigrants have family and business concerns overseas, the stability of these countries and their ties to the United States have always been sources of stress and discomfort. Combating stereotypes at home in various media has become increasingly difficult in the United States, especially since President Donald Trump's ban on visitors and immigrants from predominantly Arab states in the Middle East.

CNN reported on January 28, 2017, that "President Donald Trump's seismic move to ban more than 218 million people from the United States and to deny entry to all refugees reverberated worldwide" (Diamond and

Almasy 2017). The executive order banned citizens of seven Muslim-majority countries—Yemen, Iraq, Syria, Libya, Somalia, Sudan, and Iran—for 90 days, suspended the admission of all refugees for 120 days, and suspended Syrian refugees indefinitely. This included green card holders. Hawaii was the first state to block Trump's ban. The government then issued a new travel ban on six countries (dropping Iraq), which barred new visas for people from those countries and temporarily shut down the U.S. refugee program. The government premised its ban by stating "take a look at FDR's presidential proclamations back a long time ago, 2525, 2526, 2527. What he was doing with Germans, Italians, and Japanese because he had to do it" (Vitali 2016). The aim was to improve national security.

As the government appealed various court stays of Trump's initial ban, the public found out that the Barack Obama administration already had limited restrictions on certain travelers who had visited Iran, Iraq, Sudan, or Syria on or after March 1, 2011. Finally, on June 26, 2017, the *New York Times* reported that "The Supreme Court cleared the way on Monday for President Trump to prohibit the entry of some people into the United States from countries he deems dangerous, but the justices imposed strict limits on Mr. Trump's travel ban while they examine the scope of presidential power over the border" (Shear and Liptak 2017). Arabs and Muslims breathed a sigh of relief but only briefly. Trump then issued a list of which relationships could be considered in travel. The challenges to this part of the ban continue.

Nevertheless, chilling scenes of grandparents, daughters, sons, and fathers looking dismayed, confused, and terrorized at airports around the United States presented challenges to Arab Americans and all other Americans through continuous national broadcasting. The Trump administration had labeled all people from those countries as potential terrorists, supporters of terrorism, or relatives of terrorists; now other American citizens were seeing them that way too. Civil rights attorneys and their interns and clerks camped out in airports large and small to attempt to lessen the already paralyzing psychological blows being leveled by customs and other security agents. Some passengers had found out that they were being denied entry into the United States while they were still in the air. The psychic trauma remains.

In effect, travel bans, visa scrutiny, and potential bars to admission to countries, though not common in the West, is quite common in the Middle East, especially during times of heightened tensions between countries. Israeli citizens in general are banned from receiving general tourist visas from 13 Middle Eastern countries. Though no country bans Americans from entry based on nationality, the U.S. State Department has an ongoing and consistently updated list of travel advisories for tourists, educators, businesspeople, and so on. Several aspects of this ban are unique: its role as the fulfillment of a campaign promise made by Trump to ban Muslims from entering the country until the vetting process was straightened out, its stated intent to restrict travel from those countries with citizens involved in attacks on America, and its negligence in communication channels between security officers about who was to be denied entry.

As a world player, the United States has interests and assets everywhere, from commanders on particular battlefields to technology workers to physicians performing humanitarian feats. They too were banned. College students returning from holiday were banned or delayed. Though this state of affairs was undeniably inconvenient and life altering for some, it was more so the quickness of the rollout of the ban than the idea that a president of a sovereign state could not decide who to let into the country within the bounds of the U.S. Constitution. Arab states have been doing so for decades.

Nevertheless, the series of attempts at a ban on Muslims but not Arab Christians, who were to be rescued, solidified the Trump administration's stance as anti-Arab, anti-Muslim, and anti-Islamic. This presents a serious challenge to Arab Americans who have built and are building lives in cities across the nation.

Trying to Live an Invisible Life While Being Visible

Almost every able-bodied American works to keep self and family safe, nourished, and housed. While there is clearly a great disparity in the resources available to families by class, the particular capitalist structure of the country enables almost everyone to enjoy some semblance of luxury. Homes can be rented, leased, or purchased, as can everything from television sets to cars. These opportunities to at least experience and at most own has always made America a land to get to.

Arabs immigrated to America as a place of possibilities for their dreams but also for their survival in a time of chaos and repression. They were largely invisible because their numbers were so minute. They visibly were put into the categorization of other Mediterranean peoples and also into a demonic "other" by the vagaries of history. Immigrants at the turn of the 20th century as a group were visible because they were a teeming mass living in a section of urban life. Their clothes, languages, and ways of living further marked them as other but still insignificant. This invisible/visible state enabled many immigrants to not only find their way but also relatively thrive.

As language became a tether to the old while living in the new, most immigrants passed on language to subsequent generations along with cultural knowledge such as making food choices, tending to medical needs, and so on. If one stayed within the boundaries of the language group, one need never learn English. This happened to a number of women immigrants, especially in the Arab community. Men had to learn some English to peddle or work in factories or at other jobs. Men and children often became the more visible members of the small, insignificant, and othered Arab community. For almost the first half of the 20th century, this was the state of affairs for Arab Americans.

Even when wars broke out between Israel and various Arab states, the invisibility of Arab Americans remained. Despite plentiful news coverage of those wars and U.S. support for Israel and the oil embargo, Arab Americans remained invisible. By the time they realized the necessity of having a voice, American Jewish lobbyists had taken the floor to assert their case against Arabs. It is important to note here that not all Arabs voiced any opinion about the Arab-Israeli conflict beyond heartfelt dismay, anger, and support for any hand against them. They did not rally any part of America to their side. When visibility arrived, it was not all Arabs who become visible—only Arab Christians and Muslims who are Palestinian.

In 1948 when Israel was established as a state, Christians in Palestine made up around 18 percent of the population. Today that number is around 2 percent. A large number of Arab Christians fled or were expelled from the Jewish-controlled areas of Mandatory Palestine. Worldwide there are almost 1 million Arab Christians in diaspora. Some came to the United States and preferred invisibility. The internal politics of Arab Christians fueled the need for invisibility.

Researchers have made much note of the antipathy that Maronite (Catholic) Christians have for Palestinians, which is focused on the generally held opinion that they caused the demise of the peace in Lebanon. The Maronites are also at odds with the Orthodox communities. In the United States, however, all of their relative invisibility makes most of this moot until there is a need to continue to rescue Arab Christians from genocide. Overall, the Arab Christian community is a quiet community that seeks to educate its children, send money to the ancestral home when there is a need, and periodically educate other Americans about who they are.

Strategies of Invisibility

Arab immigrants devised several strategies for keeping cultural and religious continuity after arrival at the dawn of the 20th century, despite the fact that some were anxious to return home. Immigrant families have used many strategies to keep each generation bound to the culture. Generally, schema revolved around three or four must-haves for the Arab home.

Parents and grandparents erased much of the negative narrative surrounding the homeland. All of the features of Mount Lebanon (Greater Syria) were picturesque, as was the ability to grow one's own food, make clothing, and live closely with family. What interrupted this picture came from outside, not inside. Everyone got along with everyone else and lived side by side, and though sometimes people were of different faiths, there was little animosity. It is singular belonging, not multibelonging, that gives a human a place in the world.

Combating globality and the dislocation of migration was essential. So, families engaged in the enjoyment of and addiction to the popular culture of the Arab world. These cultures (music, fashion, dance, sports, and now cyberculture) were also modernizing, but they were still distinctively Arab as opposed to something else. Aspects of popular culture transmit political, religious, and social opinions along with expected responses to issues in both the new and old worlds. The latest fashions of the Middle East became the latest fashions of Arabs in the United States, with an American twist. Religious leaders keep control over families through their broadcasts. The influences of popular cultural connections have only increased in recent years. This situation also increases invisibility, as it tunes the senses outside of America and fits what older generations feel is necessary for cultural and religious continuity.

Religious attitudes conveyed by the first generation of Arab immigrants living in the United States have been the most stringently protected. Families are adamant about avoiding the supermarket of religious ideas that reside in Western countries, especially America. Young people are introduced to a diversity of religious and spiritual presences and practices in the United States, especially in the secular public school system. In most schools these ideas are explored without attaching belief to developing young minds. The horrors of settings such as this for immigrant parents are palpable. There are a number of venues for gender mixing, such as parties, study sessions, work, and even hospitals. Negative associations are made about other Americans, including description of loose morals.

Religious attitudes also form responses to living in America. For Arab Christians, living in the United States provided an opportunity to live outside of the Arab world and its constant persecution. Arab Muslims contend with religious dictates about living in a non-Muslim—controlled world. Islamic legal interpretations for Muslims living as minorities specifically address whether or not Muslims are persecuted or prevented from practicing their faith. Cultural and political interpretations add to the legal interpretations, foremost to keep control of a desperate population and then to gain supporters. For example, during the Arab-Israeli wars, religious leaders railed about the evils of the Israelis and the need to resist them at all costs because Islam hung in the balance. Upon migration to the United States, religious leaders railed about the inherent evils of the West and the need to maintain an Arab identity at all costs, away from the infidels.

Finally, matrimony serves to continue Arabness. Families fight an uphill battle to make sure that the next generation marries Arab. Young people born and partially raised in the United States make endless trips "back home" in part to present themselves and their citizenship as desirable. The need to integrate at some basic level for the sake of survival is muted by this driving strategy, which is several decades old for Arab Christians but recent for Muslims.

Ties to the Arab world are physical and emotional, instilled by families at very early ages. Frequent travel to sustain any remaining business or property, along with following every development in the village or city there and now easy contact by phone or Internet, has reinvigorated this aspect of the schema to keep generations tied to the Arab world. There is little if any interest in the politics or cultures of the United States unless Arabs are in some way being attacked.

Over the decades, the imagined communities in the stories of parents and grandparents have been uncovered and increasingly have to be reinvented along nationalist and religious lines to remain strong. In the United States, the imagined community is just as imagined. Immigrants associate with each other if they are from the same village, town, city, or even region. Arabness is the glue. Nevertheless, individuals are aware of the fragility of these associations while simultaneously recognizing their necessity. Even the aftermath of 9/11 could not compel many of those who were in the United States to leave and did not daunt the efforts of those trying to immigrate. It just got harder to immigrate, and now it is increasingly almost impossible except through marriage to a U.S. citizen.

One strategy of survival invisible to most Americans, but not to the Arab and Muslim community, is the proliferation of ideological organizations. Some of these organizations aim to strengthen and push for control of the cultural and political output of Arabs in America. These are purely American organizations, some of which use their ideological partners in the Arab world as funding sources. Generally speaking, they use the familiar legal resources of the United States to gain civil liberties for their communities. Other organizations strictly garner a donor base within their ethnic/

national communities to support messages to the larger American community. These strategies are certainly further nurturing the already over 100-year-old roots of Arabs in America. The United States is a place where ideology and theology and blends of both can flourish with little notice. The challenge in a multicultural, multiracial, multireligious, multiethnic society is making alliances when the major thrust is self-preservation rather than betterment of society.

Fitting either Orthodox Christianity or Islam into the religious framework of America in meaningful, contributing ways that require multiple strategies. Protesting overseas events or even attempts at genocide competes with all the other attempts at genocide or partial erasures, unfortunately. They even compete with the violence inside American society itself.

When Strategies Turn Problematic

The invisibility of Arab Christian Americans was prominently on display in remarks by Republican presidential nominee Senator Ted Cruz at a dinner sponsored by a Christian group. Given that Arab Christians often describe their plight as between a rock and a hard place, Cruz's plea for them to stand with Israel in the midst of their explaining their plight was telling of the lack of knowledge about these Christians. Cruz asserted that "If you hate the Jewish people, you are not reflecting the teachings of Christ" (Fadel 2014). Although his venom was clearly aimed at Arab Muslims and their various political groups, it just was not the time, and Arab American Christians jeered him off the stage. This incident was broadcast widely across news media. For Arab American Christians, it confirmed their invisibility. For the rest of Americans, this incident did nothing to heighten their awareness of the presence of Arab American Christians.

The landscape of America enables further invisibility for particularly small religious congregations but also facilitates uncontested space for spirituality. Several generations of Arab American Christians have grown up in particular rites, aware of other rites but unthreatened by them or by the larger Catholic and Protestant community. Orthodox churches look like any other Christian church; only the name indicates the rite and ethnic group. The interiors of Western and Eastern churches, however, are different. Again, because the difference is interior, invisibility is maintained. The safety and security of invisibility makes for little voice on issues affecting the community such as what Senator Ted Cruz was attempting to address. Invisibility means that you have no issues that concern others, and bringing you into a group means that you are malleable to the will of the majority.

Arab American Muslims, the majority in the ancestral home, became the numerical minority in the United States but by the latter part of the 20th century were the dominant voices when there was a need to have a voice. They expressed the issues and concerns of the Palestinian Arab American Muslim community rather than the issues of Arab Americans as a whole. This visibility is fraught with challenges, given the ongoing Middle Eastern wars for domination politically, economically, and religiously.

Unwanted Visibility and Its Unique Challenges

Though the Arab-Israeli wars did not catapult Arab Americans into the spotlight of American consciousness generally, the events of 9/11 did. While many immigrants found themselves under more scrutiny, those from the Arab and Muslim worlds experienced backlash in the form of intense discrimination and hate crimes against their person and places of worship, triggering various civil liberties violations.

Civil liberties are personal freedoms that the government cannot take away by law. Little of this definition held after 9/11 as Arab Americans—citizens, permanent residents, students, and H1 visa employees—were all suspect and targeted for arrest, detention, and deportation. Communities of Christian and Muslim Arab Americans were thrown into chaos. Secret detentions, selective enforcement of law through what the administration labeled voluntary interviews to obtain fingerprints, and increased intelligence gathering reminded observers of Third World military or autocratic states. Fear in Arab American communities was rampant.

Much like in the movie *Minority Report,* Middle Eastern men were rounded up for prevention rather than actual commission of a crime. Though the First Amendment attests to the fact that Americans can express opinions of all sorts in public, Arab and Muslim Americans after 9/11 found that they could be detained, questioned, and possibly jailed for any opinions regarding the demonization of their ethnic or religious group. The Fifth Amendment concerns the guarantee that American citizens cannot be deprived of life, liberty, or property without due process of law. Arab Americans found themselves detained, questioned, and sometimes jailed secretly without due process. Some even found themselves renditioned to far-off places across the world. Additionally, the category "enemy combatant" was applied without evidence, landing them in Guantánamo for indefinite interrogation.

While the Civil Rights Act guaranteed the right to protest discrimination, social and political pressures after 9/11 limited the abilities of Arab Americans to speak out against discriminatory acts. This previously invisible set of communities was wedged between forces largely outside of its American self and conflicts in ancestral homes. Arab American Muslims were the latest Arabs to come to the United States; Arab Christians had built a place for themselves, predominantly in the Midwest, and settled into the social fabric while maintaining their cultural and religious ties.

As a persecuted minority in the Middle East, Orthodox Christians are the majority Arab presence in the United States. Their plight in the Middle East was briefly highlighted by then-presidential candidate Trump: "Christians in the Middle-East have been executed in large numbers. We cannot allow this horror to continue" (Yee 2017). For many Arab Christians, a Trump presidency was a godsend in that there were promises made for their safety in the United States. The entire community of Arab Christians worked tirelessly to help in his election. After five months in office, however, the Trump administration began working to deport more than 100 men of the Chaldean Catholic community in the mix of the tens of thousands of other people rounded up as part of the clampdown on illegal immigration. Needless to say, this community is furious with the Trump administration and is imperiled as the oldest Arab American community. Arab Christians remain invisible to much of America as a religious group but quite visible to immigration and other agencies.

Arab Muslims have only increased in visibility under the Trump presidency. From campaign rhetoric to executive orders signed after Trump took office, Arabs, Muslims, and Islam have been under further attack. Arabs and Muslims became a policy category and a social target of attack. This collection of immigrants found themselves defined in terms of religion (not Orthodox Christianity, though) and ethnicity along with the deeds of a criminal few. Terms of global engagement were rewritten to ban Arabs and Muslims from the United States, and many Americans agreed. Keeping America safe now means no Arabs and no Muslims.

Overcoming the Challenges?

Attempts at climbing the uphill road to inclusion have been fraught with obstacles from both sides. The election campaign for the presidency in 2016 broke all the rules of civility and religious and ethnic tolerance. Immigrants of all ethnicities were under attack for lack of citizenship, illegal entry, and subverting the system. The American environment for

Volunteers engage in voter outreach, 2014. (Robert Nickelsberg/Getty Images)

Arab Americans was returned to an even more turbulent time than 9/11. Today the challenges only increase, as do the obstacles. Though the challenges are many, four major categories seem to encapsulate them all: issues around civil liberties, issues around inclusion, development of a scholarly literature and more widely popular literary presence across genre, and learning democratic negotiations in global communities.

One attempt at overcoming the obstacles was through an Arab American publication that sought to establish an award-winning journalistic outlet, which it has done since 1984. This publication, *Arab American News,* based in Dearborn, Michigan, focused on the rhetoric after 9/11. David Kaufer and Amal Mohammed al-Malki researched their efforts in 2009. Exploring pre- and post–9/11 stories, they found some themes that bear further examination.

At first the tragedies of 9/11 were blamed on the lack of freedom and democracy in the world, especially in Arab countries. "They hate us for our freedom" was an ongoing mantra. American women rose to save Arab and Muslim women from their despotic men and give them freedom. Literature pinpointed the speeches and utterances of the George W. Bush administration for analysis of the political field. "America will not ignore your oppression or excuse your oppressors and when you stand for liberty, we will stand with you" (Knowlton and Stout, 2005). The Arab world needed to treat its people better so they would not commit these acts of terror. To Arab Americans this was hypocritical, as they suffered the same tyranny in the United States after the first World Trade Center bombing in 1993.

The most densely populated area in the country for Arab Americans (the area around Dearborn, Michigan) found itself among the first to host a homeland security program. As Americans, they tried to comprehend the threat to the nation but also the hate-filled positioning of them as an ethnic group. Additionally, everyday Americans wanted to know about Arabs and Arab Americans, since they had changed every aspect of life. The immigration patterns of Arabs had a lot to do with their ability to handle the sudden notoriety. Arab Christians during much of the 20th century had assimilated, keeping their cultural ties. Arab Muslims who came after 1967 had already been politicized in the Arab world with nationalism. They loudly expressed their ethnic-religious identities and felt little need to assimilate.

This is one of the greatest challenges today: minority communities make themselves known not so much by their sole investment in their self-interests but instead by their critical contributions to the analysis of societal issues. Popular literature is a mainstay of American life. From romance to mystery thrillers to self-help genres, Americans are voracious in their appetites and in their recognition of new authors and compelling content. There are many ways to handle negative rhetoric beyond ongoing protests. Sometimes communities have to write themselves into the larger narratives.

Arab American literary journals rarely hit the mainstream and probably just as infrequently are consulted for opinions or attitudes regarding the treatment of this minority community. However, when Arab American writers publish in more mainstream academic journals on issues that give voice to community concerns while critiquing the rhetoric around them, a counternarrative is produced that benefits all.

This void in the American literary canon for Arab American authors, even before 9/11, inspired the first publication of the journal *Mizna,* in 1999, with the special edition title *Prose, Poetry & Art Exploring Arab America.* It was the first publication of its kind and remains the only journal of Arab American literature today. Housed in the Twin Cities in Minnesota, it now has an additional platform of a film festival.

The Self-Interests of Politics

It is a desired but unrealistic assertion that immigrant communities are averse to entering into American politics when those politics do not reflect their particular concerns. In the case of Arab Americans, the decades-old adversarial relationship between the United States and the Middle East ensures that much of American foreign policy dealing with the region will not be to the liking of the inhabitants. Nevertheless, in American political understandings, the populace has a great deal to say in support of or dissent from domestic and foreign policy. It does much of this by protest and by voting. Successful communities must have broad-issue political participation for their issues to enter the field of negotiations, which lead to consensus in global societies. No single issue should consistently dominate the agenda. An example of this kind of global negotiation exists in Hamtramck, Michigan.

Hamtramck, a small town of about 23,000 people, is almost encircled by Detroit, Michigan. For much of the 20th century, Hamtramck enjoyed notoriety as a Polish American enclave. By the end of the 20th century and the beginning of 21st century, it became a global city. It has elected a Polish-descendant mayor who governs with a Muslim-majority city council. Negotiations on jobs, housing, and city services are ongoing. Dissent is always present in democracies, but global living in democracies is the new welcomed experiment.

Profiles

Lana S. Barkaw (1974–) is a cofounder of Mizna, an organization devoted to promoting Arab American culture that has been providing a forum for its expression since 1999.

Frank Kalabat (1970–) is the first U.S.-born Chaldean to enter an American seminary. In 2001 he was elected to serve as pastor of St. Tomas Parish in West Bloomfield, Michigan, where he remains today.

References

Diamond, Jeremy, and Steve Almasy. "Trump's Immigration Ban Sends Shockwaves." CNN Politics, January 30, 2017.

Fadel, Ziad. "Dunderhead of the Year Award Goes to Texan; Big State Does It Again." *Syrian Perspective,* November 6, 2014.

Knowlton, Brian, and David Stout. "Bush Outlines Theme for Second Term: Spreading Liberty." *New York Times,* January 21, 2005.

Richards, Anne R., and Iraj Omidvar. *Muslims and American Popular Culture.* Santa Barbara, CA: Praeger, 2014.

Shear, Michael D., and Adam Liptak. "Supreme Court Takes Up Travel Ban Case, and Allows Parts to Go Ahead." *New York Times,* June 26, 2017.

Vitali, Ali. "In His Words: Donald Trump on the Muslim Ban, Deportations." NBC News, June 27, 2016, https://www.nbcnews.com/politics/2016 -election/his-words-donald-trump-muslim-ban-deportations-n599901.

Yee, Vivian. "After Backing Trump, Christians Who Fled Iraq Fall into His Dragnet." *New York Times,* July 4, 2017.

Bibliography

Abdul Khabeer, Su'ad. *Muslim Cool: Race, Religion, and Hip Hop in the United States.* New York: New York University Press, 2016.

"About Us." Arab American Family Services, arabamericanfamilyservices.org /about-us/.

"ACLU Elects First Arab America." Voice of America, https://www.voanews.com /a/a-13-2006-11-15-voa43/314246.html.

Akhtar, Mohammad, and John Esposito. *Muslim Family in Dilemma: Quest for a Western Identity.* Lanham, MD: University Press of America, 2006.

Ariens, Michael, and Robert Desto. *Religious Liberty in a Pluralistic Society.* Durham, NC: Carolina Academic Publishing, 2002.

Burch, Audra. "He Became a Hate Crime Victim, She Became a Widow." *New York Times,* July 8, 2017, https://www.nytimes.com/2017/06/08/us/he -became-a-hate-crime-victim-she-became-a-widow.ntml.

Fadel, Ziad. "Dunderhead of the Year Award Goes to Texan; Big State Does It Again." Syria in the News, November 6, 2014, www.syrianperspective.com.

Gottschalk, Peter, and Gabriel Greenberg. *Islamophobia: Making Muslims the Enemy.* Lanham, MD: Rowman and Littlefield, 2008.

Haddad, Yvonne, and Jane Smith. *Muslim Women in America: The Challenge of Islamic Identity Today.* New York: Oxford University Press, 2006.

Hajj, Abdelmajid. *Arabs in American Cinema (1894–1930): Flappers Meet Sheiks in New Movie Genre.* n.p.: CreateSpace Independent Publishing Platform, 2013.

Halaby, Laila. *Once in a Promised Land.* Boston: Beacon, 2008.

"Halal Hip-Hop: At a Time When Anti-Islamic Feelings Are on the Rise, Some Muslim and Arab-American Rappers Are Finding a Voice in the U.S." Belief Net, April 3, 2006, http://www.beliefnet.com/entertainment/music /2006/04/halal-hip-hop.aspx.

Hallaq, Wael. *Introduction to Islamic Law.* Cambridge, MA: Cambridge University Press, 2009.

Hedges, Chris. *Collateral Damage: America's War against Iraqi Civiliams.* New York: Nation Books, 2009.

Hersh, Seymour M. "Torture at Abu Ghraib." *New Yorker,* May 10, 2004, https://www.newyorker.com/magazine/2004/05/10/torture-at-abu-ghraib.

Hosseini, Khaled. *The Kite Runner.* New York: Riverhead Books, 2013.

Ignatius, David. "Trump's Reckless, Dangerous Islamohobia Helps the Islamic State." *Washington Post,* June 13, 2016, https://www.washingtonpost.com/blogs/post-partisan/wp/2016/06/13/trumps-islamophobia-helps-to-motivate-the-islamic-state/?utm_term=.86f8450e4e4a.

Jackson, Richard, et al. *Terrorism: A Critical Introduction.* New York: Palgrave Macmillan, 2011.

Jahchan, Chantal. "On Being a Christian Arab-American Woman in America." *Medium,* August 1, 2016, https://medium.com/@chantaljahchan/what-its-like-to-be-a-christian-arab-american-woman-in-america-f38861405c99.

Kahg, Mohja. *The Girl in the Tangerine Scarf.* New York: Public Affairs, 2006.

Kamal-Eldin, Tania. *Hollywood Harems: Women Make Movies.* Videocassette, 1999.

Kamali, Muhammad Hashim. *Shari'ah Law: An Introduction.* London: Oneworld Publications, 2008.

Knowlton, Brian, and David Stout. "Bush Outlines Theme for Second Term: Spreading Liberty." *New York Times,* January 21, 2005.

MacFarlane, Julie. *Islamic Divorce in North America: A Shari'a Path in a Secular Society.* New York: Oxford University Press, 2012.

Maira, Sunaina Mara. *The 9/11 Generation: Youth, Rights, and Solidarity in the War on Terror.* New York: New York University Press, 2016.

Minersville School District v. Gobitis. 310 U.S. 586 (1940).

Richards, Anne, and Iraj Omidvar. *Muslims and American Popular Culture.* Santa Barbara, CA: ABC-CLIO, 2014.

Said, Edward. *Orientalism.* New York: Vintage, 1979.

Said-Moorhouse, Lauren, and Ryan Brown. "Donald Trump Wants Extreme Vetting of Immigrants." CNN, August 16, 2016, http://www.cnn.com/2016/08/16/politics/how-us-vets-immgrants-donald-trump-extreme-vetting/index.htm.

Shaheen, Jack. *The TV Arab.* Bowling Green, OH: Bowling Green State University Popular Press, 1984.

Shear, Michael, and Adam Liptak. "Supreme Court Takes Up Travel Ban Case, and Allows Parts to Go Ahead." *New York Times,* June 26, 2017.

Sirin, Selcuk R., and Michelle Fine. *Muslim American Youth: Understanding Hyphenated Identities through Multiple Methods.* New York: New York University Press, 2008.

Stoltzius, Louis. *Amish Women.* Brattleboro, VT: Good Books, 1997.

Vitali, Ali. "In His Words: Donald Trump on the Muslim Ban, Deportations." NBC News, June 27, 2016, https://www.nbcnews.com/politics/2016-election/his-words-donald-trump-muslim-ban-deportations-n599901.

Yee, Vivian. "After Backing Trump, Christians Who Fled Iraq Fall into His Dragnet." *New York Times,* July 4, 2017.

Index

About the Author

Aminah Al-Deen, PhD, is a professor of Islamic studies in the Department of Religious Studies at DePaul University. In 2006, she was the founder of the nation's first undergraduate baccalaureate program in Islamic world studies. Al-Deen is the former editor in chief of the *Journal of Islamic Law & Culture*. Her book publications include *African American Islam* (Routledge, 1994), *Transnational Muslims in American Society* (University Press in Florida, 2006), *An Introduction to Islam in the 21st Century* (Blackwell, 2013), and, in Arabic, *Global Muslims* (2014) and *Muslim Ethics in the 21st Century* (2014), both published by Zayed University, Institute of Islamic World Studies, Dubai.

Dr. Al-Deen is a Fulbright scholar, an advisory board member of the Institute for Social and Policy Understanding, a board member of the American Islamic College, an executive board member of the Inner-City Muslim Action Network, and the American editor for the Muslim Minorities in the West series for Brill Publishers.